The Inviting Garden

The Inviting Garden

Gardening for the Senses, Mind, and Spirit

ALLEN LACY

Photographs by Cynthia Woodyard

Henry Holt and Company
New York

Henry Holt and Company, Inc.
Publishers since 1866
115 West 18th Street
New York, New York 10011

Henry Holt® is a registered
trademark of Henry Holt and Company, Inc.

Library of Congress Cataloging-in-Publication Data
Lacy, Allen, 1935–
The inviting garden : gardening for the senses, mind, and spirit /
Allen Lacy : photographs by Cynthia Woodyard.—1st ed.
p.   cm.
Includes bibliographical references (p.   ) and index.
ISBN 0-8050-3742-X (hb : alk. paper)
1. Gardens—Philosophy.   I. Title.
SB454.3.P45L335   1998   97-27539
635'.01'9—dc21

Henry Holt books are available for special promotions
and premiums. For details contact: Director, Special Markets.

First Edition 1998

Designed by Betty Lew

Printed in Hong Kong
All first editions are printed on acid-free paper. ∞

1   3   5   7   9   10   8   6   4   2

For

Samantha, Sean, and Jennifer

Anna and Sarah

May they always love to garden.

And in memory of Dr. J. C. Raulston (1940–1996)

Who left us far too soon.

Contents

PART III: GARDENING AND THE SPIRIT

Acknowledgments

A great many friends have helped in various ways during the prolonged gestation of this book. For their helpful criticism and advice, I offer my thanks to John Barstow, Martha Blake-Adams, Joanne Ferguson, and Barry Yinger—and to my agent, Helen Pratt. I must, however, single out Jo Ann White for her heroic editorial assistance at an especially crucial time in putting these pages together. As always, my wife, Hella, has been constantly supportive and remarkably forbearing.

The Inviting Garden

Preface

The gardens that have excited me the most over the years in many places in the United States, in Mexico and Costa Rica, and in Europe and Great Britain are private and personal ones, even if there's inspiration that cannot be ignored in certain famous gardens open to the public, such as Longwood Gardens, Wave Hill, Sissinghurst Castle, or the Conservatory Garden in Central Park. But all of these particular gardens, except the Conservatory Garden, were private in the beginning. The gardens I love best are those that are still affectionately tended by the people who own them and who made them—who planned and planted and replanned and replanted them, who dug in the dirt and moved hoses and watched their gardens change with the cycle of seasons and over the passage of years. A beautiful garden can be brought into being in amazingly short order by people who want it as a possession—and who have the resources to hire others to plan, plant, and tend it—but I have doubts about the ultimate worth of the enterprise. As my friend Alan Kornheiser once wrote me, "We are built, I firmly believe, to obtain clear and unalloyed pleasure only from the direct work of our own bodies. 'In the sweat of your brow will you eat your bread' is not God's curse on Adam but His blessing." Getting pleasure from a garden that is merely paid for, he went on, "implies such an incredible isolation from oneself as to invite pity." The gardens that he and I both delight in are not playthings; they are, however, places of play . . . and of work, built over time by people to whom they teach the lesson that the lines between play and work at best are not rigidly drawn.

The gardens I like best share some other things. First, they are enclosed, and second, they are inviting—in part because they are enclosed. I would not want to state categorically that a garden cannot be inviting unless it is enclosed, but I can say that I have seldom seen a garden open to the street and to public gaze that seemed to beckon, to lure me to approach for a closer look. Privacy is essential to a garden. My friend and collaborator Cynthia Woodyard makes this point quite wonderfully. "I believe in boundaries, barriers, physical and psychological," she says. "Gates, for example, give or make reason to pause before entry, preparing one for the beyond—a nice thing." She goes on to tell of the intimate joy she finds in her herb terrace, the most private spot in her garden in Portland, Oregon. There, she says, "It's warm even in winter, and I can grow tender things here. With eight lemon pots producing nicely, it's Italy. This terrace is really about food, fragrance, birds and bees—I plant with them all in mind. There is a

Cynthia Woodyard's garden in Portland, Oregon, is entirely enclosed, but its most private and secret place is the herb terrace next to the house, above a basement entryway. Here, tender tropical and subtropical plants—bananas, angels' trumpets, and potted lemon trees—mingle with sturdier plants, such as yucca, thyme, and sage.

The Woodyard terrace in summer is spectacular for its tall crape myrtles and magnificent specimens of one of the angels' trumpets, Brugmansia arborea. *There are quiet places to sit and contemplate the garden in all its lush diversity.*

wonderful little hummingbird that returns yearly, and if I sit with my head in a honeysuckle vine, he will hover very close, the closest I've come to feeling like a flower. Here, I feel as if secrets can be made and kept. I can dream and scheme, then share with the world, if I want to. How could this be done without an enclosure? Hiding beauty from the world at large may sound selfish, but gardens are an extension of our houses and ourselves, and as the world crowds in we need a private place to feed our souls or just plain hide." In speaking so engagingly for herself, Cynthia speaks for many gardeners—certainly for me.

Some of the most charming and welcoming gardens in America are concentrated in the historic district of Charleston, South Carolina. Virtually none is open to the street. At most, the passing stranger can catch only a glimpse of what lies behind their high walls of brick or their ornate wrought iron fences, although some plants spill over into public space. Roses and confederate jas-

Within its enclosure and set off from the outside world, the Woodyard garden is typified by its pyrotechnic display of contrasting and harmonizing colors and textures. Tall verbascums and lilies lift their heads above solidagos and eryngiums.

mines clamber over walls. Tall red or white or pink oleanders and yellow parkinsonia trees ascend high above walls or fences, and then arch over the sidewalk to provide a welcome touch of shade on hot days in late spring and summer. The gardens of Charleston are the very essence of the inviting garden.

An inviting garden is a garden that is a retreat from the world. It does not proclaim itself from the public street or announce its existence to passing strangers. Inviting gardens all share some other features. There will almost always be water—a small pond with fish and aquatic plants, a reflecting pool, a modest fountain. There will be animals who live in the garden, along with the human beings who enter it each day. There will surely be squirrels, probably rabbits, and possibly a raccoon or an opossum. There will be the birds that are residents year-round, the wrens, finches, cardinals, jays, and sparrows that feed on the seeds or the insects that appear in the garden according to season; and there will be the robins that leave with autumn and return with spring. There will be places to sit and to loll and to loaf, when the urge to weed or to prune has run low.

An inviting garden is one that says every morning, "Come outside. Touch, smell, taste, listen, and look. Bring your every sense with you. Brush your fingertips across the downy, silvery leaves of peppermint geranium and then breathe deeply of their fresh, delicious scent. Nibble on a leaf of chives and enjoy its mild pungency. Listen to the bird calls coming from places you cannot see, to the swishing sounds tall grasses make in the breeze, to the peepers if it's early spring, the crickets if summer is about to depart. See how the first rays of daybreak play through crimson roses, so they seem to glow from within, like stained glass. On cool days, relish the feel of the sun on your cheek, and on hot afternoons enjoy the cool, refreshing shade of the pergola over the deck. You're alive, and your garden invites you—come, enter, and linger."

In an imaginary conversation, I hear someone saying, "I want a garden just like that—an inviting garden."

I also hear the imaginary answer: "There's every chance you cannot have one, not now, not yet." Inviting gardens are mature gardens. It takes time for trees and shrubs to grow enough to offer pleasant shade to human beings and protection to wildlife. One can start immediately to make an inviting garden, but the pleasures and the rewards will be deferred—and all the more satisfying for the patient wait.

In gardening, there is only one absolute rule: *you have to garden where you are, not someplace else.* Knowing where you garden is one essential piece of knowledge. Every garden occupies a unique space. It is situated at this degree of latitude, that of longitude, at such and such a height above sea level. Latitude and longitude modified by altitude and by such geographical peculiarities as the presence or absence of large bodies of water nearby—these, taken together, impose in absolute terms the conditions under which any garden is made. They define the average length of the growing season and create reasonable expecta-

The Lacy garden on the coast of southern New Jersey has as its center a large deck on several levels that adjoins the southern and western sides of the house. Hanging baskets filled with flowering plants add color, as well as a vertical dimension. [PHOTO BY ALLEN LACY]

On the Lacys' deck, containers of both foliage plants and flowering plants provide a diverse display from early spring right up to the first frost of autumn. [PHOTO BY ALLEN LACY]

The steps of the deck are home to pots containing sempervivums and other succulents. [PHOTO BY ALLEN LACY]

tions about how harsh winter and summer will be. Other conditions are imposed by soil (whether it is clay, loam, or sand; how acid or alkaline it is; how rich or poor it is in mineral nutrients; how much organic matter it contains); by exposure; by already existing vegetation (how much shade or sun there is); and by patterns of precipitation (how much rainfall can be expected on average each year and how it is distributed through the seasons).

All of the transactions that take place in a garden are purely local. A garden is situated in a particular spot that is all its own, which not only offers opportunities but also sets limits upon what may be accomplished. There is no such

In late spring, a yellow Japanese iris called 'Aichi-no-Kagayaki' brightens the scene with its chartreuse foliage as well as its blossoms. [PHOTO BY ALLEN LACY]

thing as gardening in general; it must be done in the particular. What is universal in gardening (and it *is* universal) is the sum of a great many particulars.

Hella and I live and garden on a patch of earth just 100 by 155 feet on the coastal plain of southern New Jersey, at about 39° N of latitude and 74° W of longitude. Our garden is deeply affected by one primary fact. Its soil is extremely sandy and also well drained, because the sandy topsoil sits on a 3,000-foot layer of gravel between the tiny layer of topsoil and solid bedrock. A one- or two-inch rainfall quickly runs off, leaving the soil dry. This dryness is exacerbated during the hot months of summer by evaporation.

We cope with this problem, to the extent we are able, in several ways. All of the beds are thickly covered with mulch, which is constantly renewed. All vegetative waste, except large tree branches, is ground up with an electric chipper/shredder and then spread on the beds. All kitchen waste, except fats and meat scraps, goes into compost piles. We also buy compost from our county's recycling authority. In the past, we have also mulched with sawdust, spent mushroom soil, licorice root, cocoa shells, and marsh or salt hay. After over twenty years of regular mulching, this decomposed organic matter has altered the soil considerably, changing its color from blond to brunette and increasing its retention of moisture.

We must irrigate, of course. If we did not, we could grow only a tiny fraction of the plants that make up our garden.

The second given of our garden is that it is less than a mile from a bay of the Atlantic Ocean. New Jersey winters are sometimes mild and sometimes extremely cold. Some years there is much snow, some none. But the bay and the ocean ameliorate temperatures, warming them in the winter and cooling them in the summer. We reckon that we garden in Zone 7B. Zone 7A begins five miles to our west, and Hammonton, fewer than twenty miles from our door, is in Zone 6. We are able to grow some plants that are considered "southern"—to our delight, for they include such favorites as crape myrtles, waxleaf ligustrum, and camellias (but not, alas, gardenias, except in pots that overwinter indoors).

The third given of our garden is that it sits at the corner of two very busy roads. From the moment we moved in and were horrified by our openness to the world and to passing strangers driving by at excessive speeds, we understood that we needed privacy from the street. Obtaining this privacy has had more influence on the character of our garden than anything else. In turning it into an enclosed, private, personal space set off from the street and the rest of the public world, we have made it inviting in every sense of the word.

A snapshot of our house (which was built some time around 1812) taken from the sidewalk the first spring after Hella and I moved in shows a virtually unimpeded view stretching almost to kingdom come—all of our front yard, most of our side yard, our driveway, our back yard, our neighbor's front yard, three other front yards on the other side of the street, the yard in front of the Belhaven Middle School, an electrical substation, and the wide bicycle path that used to be railroad tracks. Nothing stopped the eye then from our front sidewalk to the oak trees beyond the bike path. Our yard contained only a few trees and precious little shrubbery. The only evidence in that photo that this old house's new owners meant to make a garden here is a small planting of daffodils blooming under the wild cherry tree at the edge of the side yard.

Another snapshot taken now from the same spot would show only the roof of the house. Everything else is obliterated from view by a thicket—a grove of tall bamboo, a tapestry hedge of roses, Virginia juniper, pyracanthas, abelias, and other woody plants, plus some miscanthuses and other massive ornamental grasses. This thicket entirely blocks any view of our garden from the front street, and it continues along the other three sides of our lot, with perhaps thirty different kinds of woody plants. We have hemmed ourselves in. When the deciduous trees and shrubs leaf out in spring, we can't see out to the street. The thicket and the mixed hedging, we might imagine, are the fringes of deep woodland that goes on for miles in all directions. Inside our thicket, on our small lot, we have made a garden, a garden specifically designed to please all the senses, each in its turn.

Gardening is restorative. It brings us back to the things we thought we had lost in childhood. It brings us back to our senses—to the downy feel of the leaves of silver sage; to the perfume of jasmines and gardenias; to the taste of spearmint; to the sound of bamboo rustling in the sudden rush of wind before a storm; to the cool white beauty of a moonflower unfolding as dusk turns into night.

But a garden is not just a retreat from the world, and there is much more to gardening than sensory delights, as important as these are. In gardening we also encounter the larger world. Gardening engages the mind in an unending quest for knowledge, for it would take many lifetimes to know and understand everything that goes on in even the smallest garden. And, finally, gardening satisfies the spirit. It connects us with a small part of the natural order that is ours to tend during our time. It involves the desire to create something of beauty. It has to do with caring and feelings of belonging to the earth. It connects us with others, for the company of gardeners is the closest thing on earth to the fellowship of saints and the communion of souls. It draws people together to become lifelong friends on the basis of a common passion for plants and affection for one another.

The pleasures of gardening are not partial, for they satisfy body, mind, and spirit. They also endure. Very few people take up gardening and then give it up because of waning interest. Whether we begin early or late, it is a lifelong commitment.

As an avid gardener, I intend this book to be an act of seduction—an introduction to the passion of gardening and its lifetime rewards. It is an invitation to the garden. I ask my readers, experienced gardeners and novices alike, to enter the world of the garden with their whole minds and souls and with every sense alive to its boundless pleasures, spiritual and intellectual as well as sensual.

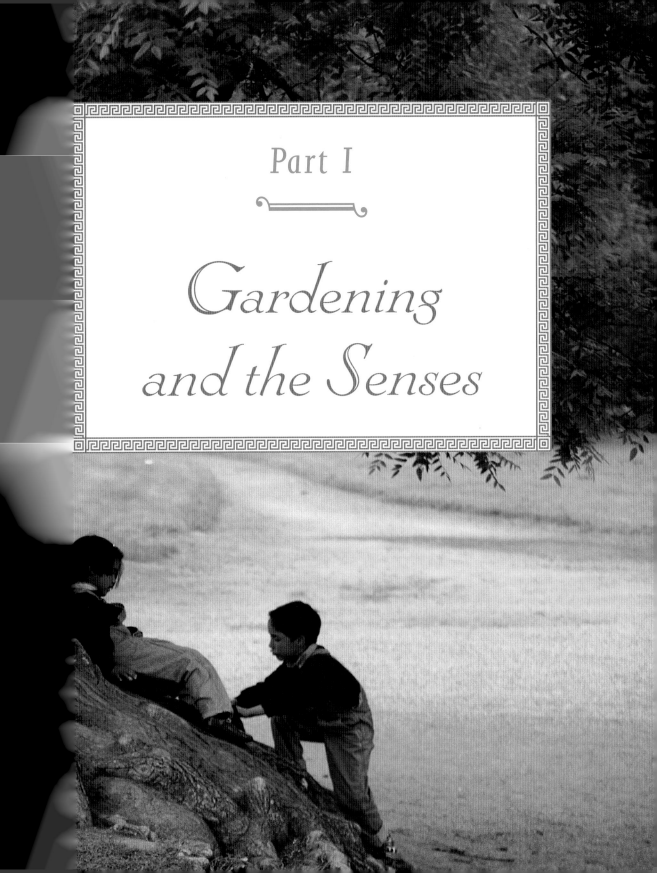

Part I

Gardening
and the Senses

Introduction

Human beings need the pleasure that comes at once to several senses, and it's hard to imagine any plant that is as pleasing to all of them as a mimosa tree. Its ferny leaves move and rustle in the slightest breeze, to a cool effect even when the temperature is in the nineties or higher. From June to August, when it is in constant bloom, its soft, silken blossoms are a glowing cerise. Stroking one or brushing it against the cheek brings voluptuous delight, the touch of eros. Their spice—so sweet you can almost taste it—travels far on warm, still summer evenings, when the leaflets fold up like tiny hands in prayer. Even though today it's plagued by disease, it weighs heavily in the memories of almost all southerners of my vintage. Whenever I catch its scent (there are a few surviving mimosas in the neighborhood), I almost feel that I'm back in Texas, and a boy again.

I write here as a gardener, but I also write as a grandparent five times over. When they visit, our grandchildren don't want to miss anything. They can't just stand in the middle of the garden and see how pretty it is. They dash forward, flying like bees to a particular flower, sticking their noses right inside to see what it smells like. They rub their cheeks against the soft satin of rose petals, and they cry out in surprise when they are pricked by a thorn. In the ancient game that all children seem to know without being taught, they pluck a honey-suckle blossom, pinch the base of the flower between thumb and forefinger, and slowly pull out the pistil until it emerges with its tiny, glistening drop of sweet

All southerners know that the mimosa tree (Albizia julibrissin) *provides gifts to every sense. Its blossoms, a silken cerise, are soft to the touch and are scented with a delicious spicy sweetness.*
[PHOTO BY ALLEN LACY]

nectar. Feasting on ambrosia, they are kin to hummingbirds—or to the gods. They want to know the name of every plant, and, surprisingly or not so surprisingly, they don't mind Latin. They notice what grown-ups fail to see—a ladybug climbing a blade of grass, a baby rabbit standing stock-still, hunched into itself, near the front of a distant flower bed. They can spend an hour dropping pebbles into a pool or swishing their hands through the water. Everything in the garden is real for them, and they want to know it, touch it, smell it, hear it, see it up close—embrace it all with their entire beings.

I hope that when they grow up, they will not lose their eagerness, their openness to discovery and surprise, their freshness to all that they see and know.

The essential thing is not so much that children should grow up (although they must), as that grown-ups should not lose altogether the innocent sensual pleasures that we knew at our beginning. We should be able to find our way back to the bright discovery days of the world as it was perceived and known in childhood, when every day brought new things to experience and to learn. We

A nna Lacy is an almost daily—and always very welcome—visitor to her grandparents' garden, a very short distance from her own home. [PHOTO BY ALLEN LACY]

should take time to smell mimosa and gardenias, too, to delight in the pleasantly felted leaves of lamb's ears, to savor the sharp spice of nasturtium leaves on the tongue, and to stand in awe as the golden slanting light of a late afternoon in midsummer plays through the the lush vegetation, illuminating first one plant and then another with a glowing radiance like that of fine stained glass. There is nothing like a garden to stimulate and satisfy each and all of our senses.

From the time we are infants, our senses develop in a steady, progressive movement from the senses of proximity and intimacy to those of distance. At each stage of this development, we enlarge the range of perception, in both distance and scope. The progression of the senses moves from the private and personal to the public and social. Touch puts us in direct contact with its objects, and

there can be few of them at any single moment. Taste also involves direct physical contact and might also be considered purely private, were it not that we
generally share meals with others of our kind. Smell has a far greater range, but
it is almost nothing in comparison with hearing. The strongest scent, whether
fair or foul, seldom travels more than a few yards from its source, but an entire
city can hear a clap of thunder. Vision is virtually infinite: half the globe sees the
sun by day, while the other half sees the moon and stars by night. Sight is our
most highly developed sense. While our vision is not as acute as it might be, it
is still our primary means of perception and knowledge once we are out of our
cribs.

Given that we are primarily visual beings, what should be the relationship
of sight to hearing and to the other, more intimate senses? In the upward
progress from touch, taste, and smell to hearing and vision, are the first three
like steps on a ladder, or are they more like the lower levels of a pyramid? If the
former, they are only stages, of minimal import once they are passed. This view
leads to a kind of asceticism: touch, taste, and smell are the animal senses, to be
transcended and even denied in the adult lives of rational beings. If, however,
the so-called animal senses are the lower parts of a pyramid, they retain their
importance even after the development of hearing and vision. We are rational
beings (at least sometimes), but we are also fully sentient beings. Vision may be
primary, but touch is primal: we never outgrow our need for it at the deepest
level of our natures as humans.

I am of the pyramid persuasion, as I think gardeners must be. The passionate gardener and the puritan can never be friends or be united in a single soul.

For reasons of convenience, the five chapters that follow take up the senses sep-
arately, although they are ultimately united in our personal lives and experience. We are fundamentally creatures of synaesthesia, beings in whom all the
senses play, on and through one another. Our simultaneous touching-tasting-
smelling-hearing-seeing finds one of its greatest satisfactions in the garden, for
gardens enrich all of the senses in their wholeness and integrity.

CHAPTER 1

Touch in the Garden

Touch is the earliest of the five senses to awaken. As newborn infants we share with our primate kin and many other mammals the primal need for the bond forged almost at birth by physical contact between mother and child. We need the assurance that comes from being snuggled and caressed, embraced and suckled.

If we were fortunate, our earliest childhood was rich in touch. Our parents played "this little piggy went to market" with us, and we squealed with delight when the game arrived at our little toe and the little pig who went *wee-wee-wee* all the way home. We got hugs and kisses. We were petted and patted. If we had trouble falling asleep, our mother rubbed our back or our head, or rocked us to the tune of a lullaby. If we were cranky and fretful, our father soothed us by holding us close and jostling us lightly as he walked around the room. We were constantly touched, and we constantly reached out to touch whatever we could get our hands on—a grandparent's glasses, our favorite stuffed animals, a warm and furry pet.

"Look, but do not touch." This lesson is learned in early childhood, often painfully. We want to avoid the business end of a wasp, the prickles of a holly leaf, sticker burs in the grass. We are taught not to touch certain things—sharp objects, electrical plugs, hot surfaces. We are taught not to be rough with pets.

We are encouraged to go easy, not to push, shove, poke, or paw. We are put on the path of becoming gentle men and women.

There is also another lesson, however: "Here, touch this; you'll like it." Stroking a cat and feeling its purr of satisfaction, rubbing the back of a dog until it smiles its doggy, panting smile—such things are vital to the education of our affections. Children ought to know the way velvet, flannel, and silk feel to the hand and the cheek. In their parents' gardens, they should be shown plants with leaves or flowers that feel like velvet or silk and be invited to touch them, to discover how they feel, not just see how they look.

"Look—but do not touch." The lesson may be learned too well if it becomes a rule of life: touch not, not ever, and be not touched. The life of a person in

Only grown-ups draw a rigid distinction between work and play. For small children, the whole world is new, and each day is a time of experimentation and exploration. Work and play meld into each other without discrimination.

whom the sense of touch has atrophied through disuse is impoverished. Such a life has lost a dimension of feeling that is crucially important not only in infancy but also to the very end of our days.

Things do not stand well with touch in contemporary America. The reasons are complex, if not difficult to fathom. In the public world, we live mostly among strangers, and the lessons of the morning paper and the evening television news are clear: every stranger is potentially dangerous. Family life, we now know, can be a far cry from *Father Knows Best*. Touch is increasingly hedged round with taboos, and many may decide to retreat from it in every form in order to avoid even the suspicion of offense. Hugs of affection and friendship are virtually an endangered species, and even the formal, perfunctory handshake becomes rarer and rarer. In certain circles, the air-kiss, a gesture of feigned intimacy, rules. As fond feelings go unexpressed in either gesture or word, our experience is inevitably diminished.

But, you may ask, what do any of these things have to do with gardening? The answer is "Plenty!" Gardens serve many purposes. One of the most crucial is the re-education of the senses, starting with touch. A garden offers, to those who accept it, a return to the touch-world of childhood.

It is sweet and pleasant to dig in the warm, slightly moist soil, to feel its grit and grain beneath the fingernails. It feels good to transplant seedlings into the ground, firming the earth around them with the fingertips or with a pat of the palms, so that they may grow and prosper. The hand of the gardener nurtures plants, but it may also root them out—with no regret in the deed. The rhythmic chore of pulling weeds soothes the soul like a mantra. No matter what the weeds, weeding also brings a feeling of accomplishment when the task is done for the day, and the doomed, partially wilted plants are hauled off to the compost heap for the eventual nourishment of the garden they tried to invade and conquer.

Weeding is handwork as is tending the soil—rolling it into a ball to see if it's ready to till or still too moist, picking out small stones, breaking up clods into small pieces. Seeds are also sown by hand: the tiny ones like begonias and petunias held in the palm of one hand while the forefinger of the other brushes them gently into their appointed places; the large ones like moonflower vines

*F*or a little boy, two sticks, a sluggish stream, and a little imagination are all that's needed in a garden for enjoyment and absorption in the business of living life to the fullest.

grasped between thumb and finger, then firmly pushed into the earth. Once the sowing is accomplished, the hands are rubbed together to remove as much dirt as possible before warm soapy water and a fingernail brush finish off the job. There's a sense of satisfaction in knowing that the work of your hands has contributed to the cultivation of the earth, helping new life come into being.

Leaf texture is largely visible, but it is also palpable. The hand may confirm what the eye sees—the leaves of silver sage and lamb's ears both look downy and feel downy. The pale, glowing green foliage of peppermint geraniums looks like velvet and feels that way, too; to see it is to wish to reach out to stroke it. But sometimes touch discovers something the eye doesn't detect. Rudbeckia foliage is as raspy as a cat's tongue. The large, paddle-shaped leaves of *Nicotiana sylvestris* are coated with a mucilaginous substance that sticks to the hand and requires soap and water to remove; a close inspection of the back of the leaves shows that this coating traps and immobilizes small insects. Cleome leaves are clammy, also prickly. The enormous leaves of paulownia seedlings are so downy

An ancient tree at Versailles is a shady haven for rest and relaxation, an invitation to adventure for the daring.

as to feel almost furry, and the unripe seed pods of the tree are unpleasantly sticky.

One summer day in my garden, a small red Japanese maple gave me a surprise. It and a gray santolina were encroaching on each other, so I grabbed some shears and removed a bit of each, throwing the clippings on the warm sidewalk nearby. When I picked them up to take to the compost heap, the slightly wilted maple leaves had the soothing feel of well-worn suede. Sometimes, of course, the same plant offers contradictory testimony of itself to the touch. Such peculiar sensory dissonance occurs with the huge, murderously armed silver leaves of the Scotch thistle. It looks very prickly, and indeed the spines on the edges of the leaves easily pierce a finger and bring a drop of blood. But the leaves along their central veins are as soft and smooth as satin.

Flowers and fruits have their tactile qualities, too. Rose petals caress the cheek with their silk, and the flowers of magnolias and gardenias feel wonderfully of soft leather, although they turn brown where they have been touched.

The downy, unripe fruits of quinces delight the fingers, as do the smooth and waxen ones of ripe pomegranates. The heft of an apple pleases the hand that holds it.

We need the rough as well as the smooth. We may benefit from knowing that everything is not always to our pleasure: thus spines, prickles, thorns, and stickers teach their valuable lesson of touch-me-not. Tree bark, in all of its great variety, is irresistible. So, in fact, are trees, when they have grown to great dimension. When I touch one of the live oaks of the coastal Carolinas that was already immense when Columbus set sail westward, I turn Druid. Live oaks spend a century or more growing upward, in the manner of most trees. But in their later centuries, ponderous with weight, they grow outward and downward. Their enormous swooping branches come close to the ground, offering an invitation to grab hold and climb up. The grown-up will probably decline the invitation, for we have learned to aspire little, to seek no adventure in the arms of a majestic, venerable tree.

In autumn, the seed pods of two remarkable plants bring a marvelous surprise to the inquiring hand when they have fully ripened and are lightly touched! Impatiens gets its name from the sudden explosion that hurls its seeds in every direction. Children laugh with glee when they touch the pods and

In the celebrated rose garden of Montisfont Abbey near Salisbury, England, no rule prohibits walking on the grass—or exchanging a hearty embrace, either.

Magnolia campbellii combines a sweet lemony fragrance, great beauty of form, and petals with the texture of fine suede.

bring about this vegetative pyrotechnics. The squirting cucumber (*Ecballium elaterium*) is even more noteworthy, as its fuzzy, pale-green seed capsules, shaped like little footballs, go ballistic—in keeping with this plant's genus name—sailing high in the air, propelled by a jet of water spewing from the stem end of the fruits.

The language of botany, concerned primarily with the visible and the measurable, does attend to the tactile qualities of certain plants. If its species name is *spinosus*, it has spines; if *aculeatus*, it's well furnished with prickles; if *inermis*, it's unarmed—has neither spines or prickles. If its species name identifies it as *pilosus*, its leaves are covered with short, thin hairs; if *pubescens*, downy; if *incanus*, it is so covered with dense, short hairs as to appear white. A species that is *velutinus* is velvety to the hand; *lanatus*; woolly; *sericeus*, silken. Beware of anything described as *urens:* it stings.

Before we were *Homo sapiens*, humanity capable of rational intellect and choice, we were *Homo erectus*, humanity standing upright on two feet, holding in our hands axes and other stone tools of our own making. The use of tools continues to define us as human.

Today, my thoughts and the observations of my five senses appear on a screen as I tap my fingers on a computer keyboard, but in the garden, I am comfortable with the tools that descend directly from those my *Homo erectus* ancestors devised, knew, and used. My shovel and my spade turn the earth, making it habitable for the plants I choose to grow. My shears and my loppers enable me to prune plants according to their needs and my intentions. A dandy little Felco saw that cuts precisely on both the forward and backward strokes of my arm transmits the feel of biting into something real—the wood of a branch that grows where I would not choose it to grow.

Besides the touch that comes through the hand and the use of tools, there is also the more diffuse touch that comes through the whole body, encased in its protective skin. The organ of touch is not just the hand but the entire skin, the largest organ of the body. What it perceives it perceives directly, and what it knows it know with the utmost intimacy. Tactile pleasures—and also pains—are the most intense of all perceptions. All talk of the pleasures of touch verges on and even transgresses into the world of eros. It is no accident that Lady Chatterley's lover was a gardener.

It is a sensual joy to walk barefoot on sun-warmed or dew-drenched grass. No grown-ups ever quite forget the mud pies and sandpiles of their early childhood, back in that time when make-believe was part of the very grain and substance of reality. (Grandchildren make a fine excuse for relearning the pleasures of soft, gooey mud, of sharp sand with its gritty feel and sound—and for returning to make-believe.)

We not only touch things, but things also touch us. As we stand in the sun, a ladybug lands on our arm and takes a stroll through a forest of hair. We lie half asleep in a hammock, and a raindrop falls on our forehead. A sudden storm breaks out, and before we can dash inside we are drenched to the skin.

A nesting bird, alarmed at our approach, flies out of a shrub in a great rush, the tip of a wing brushing past our head. An old cat, dozing in the sun, awakens, stretches, and idles over to brush against our legs, purring with obvious well-being. The sun warms our cheeks and the back of our necks, or a sudden chilly breeze makes us shudder. We walk down a little garden path at night and brush aside the spiderwebs spun to catch less wary prey.

Sun and shade also touch us. They are generally considered to be primarily visual experiences, phenomena of light and darkness, and so they are for the

A garden, for a cat, is rich in things to touch, as well as to see, hear, and smell.

When autumn arrives, the spiders that have been busy since spring spangle the landscape with their gleaming silvery webs.

eye, but the whole body senses them as well. Sun on the cheek is welcome on a cool day; shade when it's hot refreshes and cools. Gardens may have their corners where it's sunny all day long if the sky is not overcast, and they may have their nooks of perpetual shade. But sun and shade are usually movable feasts, alternating with each other in harmony with the progress of the sun from horizon to horizon.

And always, as we walk, we feel the ground under our feet—and we know that we are at home here on our own patch of earth, at home here in our garden.

CHAPTER 2

Scent in the Garden

Fragrance is the strongest and most mysterious of the sensual pleasures that gardens offer. Anyone who has ever breathed deeply of the large ivory chalices of our native southern magnolia and savored their sharp and lemony sweetness on the cusp of summer, or broken open one of the tree's bright red seeds in October, thus perfuming the hand with the bracing scent of bay rum, knows that it is good to be alive. The odor of wisteria blossoms on the night air in late spring, commingled with the sweeter scent of honeysuckle vines, is never to be forgotten, once experienced. Indeed, as many people have noticed, fragrance is connected in the most intimate way with memory. Smell, if we surrender to it, puts us in touch not only with the *now,* but with the *then.* It allows us to live fully in the present, accepting the rich, sweet, penetrating perfumes of gardenias, jasmines, ripened grapes, and other deep scents of the earth, while also opening a doorway that leads backward into days thought lost. This association of smell and memory has so often been remarked that it would be a cliché, were it not so deep a truth. Each of us has our talisman fragrances, odors that magically obliterate the intervening days and years between ourselves as we are now and ourselves as we once were.

For Helen Keller, this fragrance came from the mimosa tree, about which I have already put in a word. Writing in *The Story of My Life* (1903), when she was in her early twenties, she recalled the seventh summer of her childhood in Alabama, when she suddenly caught a delicious, subtle fragrance in the air.

What is it? I asked, and the next minute I recognized the odour of the mimosa blossoms. I made my way through a shower of petals to the great trunk and for one moment stood irresolute; then, putting my foot in the broad space between the forked branches, I pulled myself into the tree. . . . I sat there for a long, long time, feeling like a fairy on a rose cloud. After that I spent many happy hours in my tree of paradise, thinking fair thoughts and dreaming bright dreams.

Helen Keller could not have known that there might come a time when a child in the South might not grow up with the scent of mimosa flowers engraved in the brain. Mimosas are in trouble wherever they grow from a vascular wilt disease that condemns them to a prolonged and ugly demise. The time may come when they will pass away from the world of remembered fragrances. This is a true loss, for Helen Keller was by no means unique in finding their spicy sweetness a passageway into deep memory.

I am saddened by the decline of the mimosa, for its scent is my own talisman. One whiff of its delicate perfume on the evening air brings back all the warm bodily confusion of those days when I was ceasing to be a child but was not yet a man, and would read myself to sleep at night intoxicated by the almost palpable fragrance of mimosa blossoms.

Fragrance, we have been told time and again, is notoriously subjective, and because it is so, disagreements arise among us about whether the scents of particular plants are pleasant and agreeable or are not. Boxwood is perhaps the chief example. We are so divided in our response to the odor of boxwood hedges, particularly right after a rain on a warm summer day, that the division may be coded in our genes. People love it or hate it, and no one seems to be neutral or undecided. In *The Fragrant Path* (1932) Louise Beebe Wilder gave equal attention to both sides without revealing her own affiliation: "Like the Sweetbriar its young leaves give off an especially keen fragrance after a shower of rain, when many persons find it oppressive and vaguely disturbing." When British writers get round to the subject of boxwood, they usually remind us that Queen Anne found it so distasteful that she had all of it removed from Hampton Court. I am of the queen's party. When I smell it in someone else's garden I always think I have stumbled on a urinal for cats.

Other plants with fragrance that the great majority of us consider highly agreeable may nevertheless find resistance on the part of a few. It almost passes understanding, but even roses and their fragrance have had their detractors. Anne of Austria, wife of Louis XIII of France, had such an aversion to roses that she could not stand seeing one even in a painting. But she represents a tiny minority. Roses are almost universally loved, and the stronger the scent, the deeper the affection.

Many of the formal gardens of Charleston, South Carolina, smell strongly of boxwood. At Avalon, on Church Street in the city's historic district, clipped hedges of box define the garden's structure, their scent mingling with that of rosemary.

Mention fragrant flowers, and the first thing most people will think of is roses. This cultivar is 'Mrs. Oakley Fisher'.

People may also divide on those lilies that have pronounced scent, like Madonna lilies, Easter lilies, regal lilies, and the late-blooming Oriental hybrids. I find their heavy, pervasive, sweet spiciness completely delectable, but others—Colette comes to mind—demur, holding them to be cloying, funereal, almost sickening. There are also rare individuals who do not like the generally beloved sweet fragrance of mock orange, including the great seventeenth-century herbalist John Gerard. In *The Herball* (1633), he wrote of the flowers of mock orange that

> in my judgement they are too sweet, troubling and molesting the nose in a very strange manner. I once gathered the floures and laid them in my Chamber window, which smelled more strongly after they had lien together a few houres, with such an unacquainted savor that they awaked me out of my sleep, so I could not take my rest till I had cast them out of my chamber.

Many people—and I am one—would of course disagree with Gerard about mock orange, the various hybrid cultivars of *Philadelphus.* These large, rangy, and fairly untidy bushes, which take their common name from the use of their flowers in England as a substitute for orange blossoms in bridal bouquets, are covered with four-petaled white blooms in late May. I have two mock oranges, planted close to the house so that they may waft their heavy perfume through windows flung open to catch the spring breeze. For the week—more or less, depending on how warm the weather is—that mock orange is in bloom, it is a gift to the nose and to the soul, for its fragrance is sweet, clean, and refreshing.

The subjectivity of scent also shows itself in disagreements about whether a particular plant has any odor at all (I have friends who claim that oakleaf hydrangeas have a delicate but lovely scent, but I cannot detect even a trace), and in disagreements about what plants that *do* have an odor smell like. Take our native Carolina allspice (*Calycanthus floridus*), which comes into its long period of bloom on the verge of summer. Its flowers smell agreeably like ripe fruit—to my nose, strawberries in the hot sun of noon, but there are other opinions. Rosemary Verey thinks they smell like ripe apples. In *Old-Time Gardens* (1901), Alice Morse Earle wrote: "I have often tried to define to myself the scent of the Calycanthus blooms; they have an aromatic fragrance somewhat like the ripest Pineapples of the tropics, but still richer; how I love to carry them in my hand, crushed and warm, occasionally holding them tight over my mouth and nose to fill myself with their perfume." It needs to be noted about the Carolina allspice, however, that sometimes instead of disagreements about what it smells like, there is agreement that it has no odor at all: the degree of fragrance in the flowers of this small shrub is genetically determined, and some seed-grown specimens lack scent altogether.

I believe that we should make our gardens as fragrant as possible over as long a season as possible. This point would seem to be so obvious that it hardly needs to be made at all, except that our habits—and the way that plants are marketed today—conspire against the achievement of this goal. The woody plants, bulbs, perennials, and annuals that are staples of the nursery and garden center trade tend strongly toward a total absence of scent. Hybridizers of tea roses have not made fragrance a consistent criterion in their work, although very recently there has been some improvement here. Wholesale seed companies have done remarkable things with bedding plants like petunias and impatiens in regard to improvements in color selection and a prolonged season of bloom, but they have overlooked our sense of smell altogether. Accordingly, those of us who place special value on gardens that are as fragrant as possible must select our plants with this end in mind.

I see no need to speak out on behalf of the sweet-smelling hyacinths and jonquils, lilacs and mock orange, roses and lilies that are so well-known and common. But we can go farther down the perfumed path.

Far too often in choosing the woody plants that are the backbone of any garden, we fail to take scent into consideration. In choosing small trees, for example, we may plant Japanese flowering cherries, which bloom beautifully but briefly in mid-spring—a time of year when the garden is so plenteous with bloom that the absence of cherry trees would hardly even be noticed. We might turn instead to a wonderful pair of plants that bloom for many weeks, not in spring, but in winter—one in midwinter, the other at its end—when their flowering would be cause for rejoicing even if they had no more scent than a scrap of cardboard. I mean the hybrid witch hazels, such as 'Arnold Promise', and *Prunus mume,* the flowering Japanese apricot. Neither is as widely known or as widely planted as it deserves.

Hybrids of the Asian species *Hamamelis mollis* and *H. japonica,* the witch hazels bear flowers whose ravishing scent of honey and allspice carries with it a sensuousness that seems unsuited to ascetic winter. 'Arnold Promise' blooms profusely from early January to the end of February, with wispy golden flowers that are extremely beautiful when backlit on a sunny morning. A small branch brought inside perfumes an entire room with its rich, heady fragrance. Other, equally fragrant cultivars include 'Jelena' (coppery red), and 'Pallida' (lemony yellow). The very existence of these wonderful small trees is something of a secret to many. Garden centers don't sell them, for the simple reason that they bloom when garden centers aren't yet open, and wouldn't have customers if they were open. Still, if people chance to see them in bloom, brightening up the dim days of winter, they want them—and all the more if they realize how sweet and powerful their scent is.

The hybrid witch hazels (Hamamelis × intermedia) *are among the most fragrant of all shrubs, and all the more valuable because they bloom over a long period in the dead of winter, as is obvious here with the cultivar* 'Arnold Promise'.

Prunus mume is a flowering apricot native to Japan, where its blossoms—frequently misidentified by Westerners as plum blossoms—are a common motif in traditional painting and pottery. The single or double flowers in March may be red, pink, or white. They are heavily scented of almonds, with an overtone of baby powder. There is no lovelier sight than this apricot tree in full bloom on a morning after heavy snow has fallen on a calm, windless night, when the blossoms glow from within their coating of crystalline white.

Among herbaceous plants, several bulbs lend fragrance to the winter air, beginning with snowdrops (*Galanthus nivalis*). In my garden, true to their name, they come into bloom in January, when their pendant, nodding, milky-white flowers are sometimes encased in snow and ice. But their delicate scent may go undetected unless they are brought inside to warmth. They're not especially suited to be cut flowers, of course, and it's a pity to deprive the garden of flowers in this time of year when bloom is so precious. The same thing is true of another tiny charmer, *Cyclamen coum*, with its little butterfly flowers of magenta, rose, or white rising only an inch or two above the mounds of dark green or pewter variegated rounded foliage. The fragrance is there, but it's faint, and it seems unfair somehow to pluck the flowers.

One of the choicest fragrant plants of late winter is the Algerian iris, which Elizabeth Lawrence described as follows in *A Southern Garden* (1942):

> Of all winter flowers the Algerian iris, *Iris unguicularis*, is most to be desired for delicacy of texture and coloring, and for fragrance. . . . I like to think of the grey morning when I found one in bloom for the first time in my garden, in an otherwise desolate border. The plants had been flowerless for so many seasons that I had not only ceased to hope, but had also forgotten their very existence. I can think of nothing so bright and fragile as this iris, nor so fragrant when it is brought indoors to warmth. It has been described as smelling of violets, and again of primroses. To me it smells of spring.

There is a fine paradox here, of course—a winter-blooming plant that "smells of spring." It may also be noted that for that indoor fragrance the flowers of the Algerian iris must be picked just before they open. Other irises also smell delicious. *Iris reticulata,* probably better considered a very early spring bloomer rather than a winter one, has a most distinctive scent—violets and ripe grapes! The grape odor appears again in some—not all—bearded irises when they bloom in late spring, and the scent of other fruits belongs to other irises. *Iris pallida* is reminiscent of apricots, *Iris persica* of apples.

April brings the intense scent of the hardy orange, *Poncirus trifoliata,* a small tree or large shrub that is fully winter hardy to coastal Massachusetts. Close kin to lemons, limes, and oranges, although not in their genus, *Citrus,* the hardy orange exceeds even roses in combining sublime fragrance with vicious armament. The perfume of its single, waxy, pure white flowers is indistinguishable from that of orange blossoms, but the plant is guarded by a multitude of large, exceedingly sharp thorns, so formidable that a hedge of the plant surrounding a garden will guarantee that no two- or four-legged trespasser can ever get in. The fruits in autumn look like little oranges but are bitter and inedible. The plant defoliates in winter, but its stems (and thorns) remain bright

Some bearded irises have a delicious grapelike scent, but others do not. An exploratory sniff will settle the question, as here in the iris garden at Bagatelle in Paris.

green and attractive. (It must be noted that hardy oranges, like calycanthus, vary in fragrance. The occasional plant may lack scent altogether.)

One of mid-spring's richest perfumes belongs to the blossoms of the empress tree, *Paulownia tomentosa*. It grows phenomenally fast, up to eight feet a year if it's happy, and it doesn't take much to make a paulownia happy. Its huge clusters of large, foxglove-like, pale lavender and cream blossoms, appearing in May before the leaves, are strongly and pleasingly scented with a perfume of ambrosia and apricot. As the tree ages, the flower clusters may bloom out of reach, but it doesn't matter: the extremely pervasive fragrance carries far on the spring air for a week or more. Even the spent flowers that fall to the ground are deliciously scented. An empress tree allowed to grow in its own way is lovely in every season. The fragrant flowers are followed by clusters of slightly clammy yellowish-green fruits that look like enormous grapes. The fruits persist on the trees all winter, turning brown and opening halfway so that they resemble little boats. (Children love to float them.)

Of the four seasons, spring is by far the wealthiest in agreeable scents. Some plants advertise themselves forcefully, with fragrances that carry far. Thus it is with stocks, wallflowers, daphnes, clove currant, and many dianthus, including sweet William. In the South, where it is winter hardy, gardeners can revel in the intoxicating odor of *Michelia figo,* whose common name, banana shrub, names it precisely: gardens where it grows are redolent of ripening bananas for over a week. Others—lily of the valley, sweet violets, and grape hyacinths among them—must be brought to the nose to relish their delectable odors.

With summer's advent, a number of annuals also arrive to perfume the air. Sweet alyssum (*Lobularia maritima*) is an engaging little plant, often used as an edging for herbaceous borders or paths. It comes in a variety of pastel colors, but the fresh scent, much like new-mown clover, is most pronounced in white strains. Plants of sweet alyssum are among the common staples of garden centers, but most of the truly choice fragrant annuals don't turn up in such places, for they either dislike being transplanted or take their own sweet time in blooming. They have to be raised from seed, as our grandmothers grew them. (Our grandmothers had to raise everything from seed, and as a result they grew many more kinds of annuals than are common today.) Among such annuals, I have some favorites. Dame's rocket (*Hesperis matronalis*), a cottage-garden favorite in England since the sixteenth century, takes its genus name from the Greek word for evening (the same word that gives us "vespers"), because the scent of its modest flowers in shades of lavender and purple intensifies as dusk comes on. Also notable for its nighttime perfume (think jasmine with overtones of lime and cinnamon), the evening stock (*Matthiola longipetala*) is unprepossessing, even dowdy, in flower, but its scent redeems it and earns it room in the garden—ideally, a place near a window that is open at night, the more to enjoy its unmistakable incense. Both of these annuals must be grown from seed, but a single planting is enough, for they will readily volunteer from then on.

I can't imagine a summer without the delicate spice of nasturtiums, or summer's end without moonflower vines, entirely handsome creatures, with deep green, glossy, heart-shaped leaves. The flower buds grow quickly into spiraling tapers that swell and balloon at dusk into pure white saucers whose faint but delicious perfume draws nocturnal moths to sip their nectar. Until frost comes, each night there are more and more flowers.

I could not live comfortably without flowering tobaccos, although hybridizers have largely deprived the bedding hybrids derived from *Nicotiana alata,* the jasmine tobacco, of any trace or suggestion of jasmines. The best flowering tobacco by far is *N. sylvestris,* the woodland tobacco from Argentina. A fine plant either for the mixed border or for pot culture on decks or patios, it rises in a pyramid as much as five feet above its enormous pale green lower leaves. Its pure white, long tubular blossoms are pyrotechnic, exploding in a circle in tiered whorls at the top of sturdy, branching stems. Its delicious scent grows

The most fragrant of the flowering tobaccos is the woodland tobacco of Argentina, Nicotiana sylvestris—*one of the most imposing and dramatic plants of the late summer and early autumn garden. It is a prolific self-seeder: plant it once, and you'll delight in it year after year.*

stronger at night, when the somewhat drooping flowers lift upward to greet the moths that are their pollinators.

Once common in gardens and among their most powerful sources of perfume, mignonette (*Reseda odorata*) is planted very seldom these days. It offers little in the way of visual appeal, being somewhat weedlike, but it has a long and illustrious history. Native to the southern Mediterranean basin, it was used in the Egypt of the pharaohs as a medicinal plant. Pliny gave it its Latin name, from *redo*, meaning "I calm," and the Romans used it in an ointment for bruises. Its common name is French, meaning "little darling," but the name dates only from the early eighteenth century, when the plant became extremely popular in France. The English adopted the craze in the 1740s, growing mignonette in pots to be brought indoors when it came into flower, bearing racemes of tiny, fairly nondescript white and yellow flowers with a fragrance that Philip Miller's *The Gardener's Dictionary* (1731) described as "like fresh raspberries." The popularity of mignonette extended into Victorian times and well beyond, in America as well as Europe.

Thomas Jefferson grew mignonette at Monticello, regularly ordering seeds from Bernard M'Mahon, a noted Philadelphia nurseryman. Jefferson obviously had a keen appreciation for scent in his garden, for he also ordered from M'Mahon two other highly fragrant plants, one a tuberous subtropical herb native to Mexico, the other a tender perennial from Peru, that are today considered to be old-fashioned favorites, like mignonette. They were tuberoses (*Polianthes tuberosa*) and heliotrope (*Heliotropium arborescens*).

Jefferson evidently loved Mexican tuberoses, recording in his garden notebook on April 18, 1806, that he had planted twenty-four double ones from M'Mahon. They started flowering on August 12, and the following January Jefferson placed a larger order with M'Mahon, who wrote back on February 25 that the shipment would be delayed: "When the weather becomes more mild I will send you some double Tuberose roots, but as they are extremely impatient of frost, it would be hazardous to send them at present."

As for heliotrope, Jefferson discovered it in France during his diplomatic career there. In 1786, he sent seeds to his grandson, Francis Eppes, instructing him that they should be "sowed in the spring, planted in boxes & kept in the house in the winter." "The smell," he noted, "rewards the care."

The scent of heliotrope still "rewards the care." It is also particularly associated with the awakening of ancient memories. Rosetta Clarkson writes in *Green Enchantment* (1940) that:

> The odor of heliotrope, more than any other plant, can surround me with memories of other days, other times; can stir my imagination to scenes of dainty ladies, receiving courtly gentlemen to afternoon tea, of an opera party in the 'nineties with the guests in full regalia assembling in the box overlooking the stage. There is something intoxicating about the odor and as I bury my nose again and again in the fragrant clusters, more memories, more scenes crowd about me.

Both Jefferson and Clarkson remark on heliotrope's fragrance, without being specific about it. One of the plant's common names, cherry pie, tells the tale, for at its best it smells just like cherry pie tastes. But with heliotrope the rule is sniff before you buy, for its scent is highly variable, and one of the variations is no scent whatsoever. Heliotrope also varies in color, ranging from dark purple to deep blue to lavender to pink and white. English gardeners can choose from a large number of vegetatively propagated cultivars of assured fragrance, but none of these seems as yet to have reached our shores. Hardy only to Zone 10 and parts of Zone 9, heliotrope does not winter well inside, Jefferson's advice to Francis Eppes notwithstanding. It must be sought out in bloom at local nurseries or greenhouses, always with that investigative sniff.

Summer has its fragrant shrubs as well as annuals. Among them, buddleias are indispensable for their wide range of color, their long season of bloom, their resistance to disease, and, not least, their fragrance of honey and ripe blackberries. Whoever came up with "butterfly bush" as the common name for these plants was not particularly poetic or even observant: monarchs and skippers and swallowtails flit in virtual clouds around the long spikes of bloom, seeking out their nectar and adding their own colors to those of the flowers, which

Butterfly bush is an almost inevitable common name for the several species of Buddleia *and their many hybrids. This long-blooming summer shrub, notable for its spicy blackberry scent, is a magnet for butterflies attracted by its abundant sweet nectar.*

range from white to pink to crimson and purple, and even intense metallic shades of blue-violet.

Buddleias bloom most of the summer, well into fall, but the native American shrub *Clethra alnifolia,* commonly called sweet pepperbush, waits until August to put in its word. It does not smell like pepper; this part of its name comes from the little specks of brown at the center of its tiny cream-colored or pale pink flowers. In my part of the world, you don't have to grow sweet pepperbush to delight in its fragrance, for it comes borne on the wind, from roadside ditches, the edges of marshes, and other moist spots in the neighborhood. You can't drive through the countryside in late summer hereabouts without enjoying the spice of clethra. I can't describe the scent by comparing it with anything else, for it is distinctive, something that belongs to itself alone.

Two more woody plants deserve mentioning. It's not hardy much north of Philadelphia, but *Elaeagnus pungens,* the thorny elaeagnus, disperses into the air a powerful scent reminiscent of gardenias late in October. And one of the most exciting new plants to come along in this waning century is *Heptacodium miconioides,* which is rare even in its native China. Grown at the Arnold Arboretum and the National Arboretum of the USDA from seeds collected in China in 1980, it is only now beginning to be discovered by gardeners. It bears sprays of jasmine-scented white flowers in September, followed by reddish-purple bracts that stay till frost. Everyone who has seen it and smelled its flowers predicts that it will become hugely popular.

Although some sweet-smelling plants, such as mignonette and heliotrope, are pretty much constant bloomers from late spring into fall, the fragrance of flowers during the growing season is largely an ever-changing affair. Mock oranges make their appearance and then fade from the scene as roses come into the limelight. Sweet pepperbush comes on as Oriental lilies drop their last petals of the year. But some good, bracing, and pleasant odors are constant presences during the entire green year, although they intensify in late summer, when the combination of hot afternoons and increasingly cooler evenings serves to intensify the strength of the essential oils contained in their foliage, to make them speak with greater authority. These are the odors of the scented foliage found in a number of plants, culinary and medicinal herbs in particular.

A few plants with scented leaves proclaim themselves unmistakably as the volatile molecules of the essential oils they contain evaporate into the atmosphere. Lavender makes no secret of itself. Neither does the most delicious-smelling species of all the basils, holy basil (once *Ocimum sanctum,* now *O. tenuifolium*). If you but touch it, its indescribable spice will fill the air for many feet around, and also linger on your hand for hours.

Another plant with powerfully scented leaves is *Helichrysum italicum.* It is almost hoydenish in announcing its presence from a considerable distance before the plant is seen. Its common name, curry plant, names its aroma exactly, which is fairly peculiar, considering that curry powder is a human concoction, a compound of five essential elements—the seeds of coriander, cumin, and fenugreek, the rhizome of turmeric, and the dried fruits of cayenne pepper. That a single herb should also produce the distinctive odor of curry is as remarkable as some new rose coming into bloom with the exact fragrance of Chanel No. 5 or Opium.

The greater number of plants with scented leaves do not generally release their fragrance into the air. They must be crumpled, crushed, trodden on, or at least brushed against to reveal their odor, and their odor is always a surprise on

The terrace garden at Gravetye Manor is a symphony of fragrance as well as color, but the predominant scent is that of the lavender that has been planted with a generous hand.

first encounter. There is no way that you can look at the Florida anise tree (*Illicium floridanum*) and know that its bruised foliage smells like anise or licorice (although you might have a hunch if someone first tells you its common name). Nor can you look at sweet goldenrod (*Solidago odora*) or anise hyssop (*Agastache foeniculum*) and know in advance that the leaves conceal a similar evocation of anise.

The one group of plants with scented leaves that virtually everyone knows, whether he gardens or not, are the true mints, species in the genus *Mentha*. All have delightfully piercing fragrance, even if only barely touched. No garden should be without its spearmint (*M. spicata*), whose crushed leaves in iced tea (also in bourbon whisky, as a julep) refresh body, mind, and soul on hot days. Apple mint (*M. suaveolens*) and orange mint, a varietal form of peppermint (*M. × piperita*), are both deliciously scented, and their common names suggest their fruity notes and overtones. Corsican mint, or crème de menthe plant (*M. requienii*), would be practically indispensable, were it winter-hardy, as it is not except in Zone 10 and parts of Zone 9. It is a tiny, creeping thing, a mere green film on the ground, and it smells exactly the way the liqueur that's made from it tastes.

Other members of the Labiatae, or Mint family, are not true mints, but they mimic spearmint. One is the North American native mountain mint, *Pycnanthemum tenuifolium,* a rather lax and sprawling plant, which has attractive little glossy leaves that smell of spearmint, and a heavy, foamy-looking crop of tiny pinkish-white flowers borne in clusters in late summer and early autumn. Another is a calamint, *Calamintha nepeta,* which again has a scent quite close to that of spearmint. The mounded, tidy plants put up spikes of tiny white flowers with a lavender cast. *Calamintha nepeta* is variable in the nursery trade. It is worth seeking out the subspecies *C. n.* ssp. *nepeta,* which has smaller and glossier foliage than the straight species and also does not seed itself around the garden in a troublesome way.

You can't cook with a calamint, but you can, and probably do, with basil and thyme, both of which have many forms. The match between common basil and tomatoes as a treat for the tongue was made in heaven (well, Italy), but other basils delight the nose, including ones that smell of anise, cinnamon, and lemon. These are upright annual herbs, but thymes are mostly prostrate perennials. Their habit makes them well suited for growing between flagstones or stepping-stones on a sunny walkway, where their aromatic oils may be released by radiant heat, as well as the occasional wayward footfall. Some smell only of thyme, itself a potent scent, but others have overtones of caraway, coconut, lemon, nutmeg, and orange.

The grand champions among plant pretenders with foliage suggestive of the smells of other plants are the scented-leafed pelargoniums, which have been grown and collected since the seventeenth century. They offer a veritable potpourri of fragrances. At least twenty-five cultivars smell of roses; almost as many of lemon. Other scents include almond, apple, cedar, chocolate mint, coconut, filbert, ginger, juniper, lime, nutmeg, orange, peppermint, pine, spearmint, strawberry, and even Old Spice aftershave lotion.

Gardens and kitchens have something in common. They are, or ought to be, filled with good odors. In both kitchens and gardens, we may find smells that delight us, that remind us of good things in the past and that fill our souls in the present with a sense of well-being. But there's a huge difference between the smells of the kitchen and those of the garden, even though in both we may speak of spice and vanilla, cloves and honey, lemons and almonds.

What we smell in a kitchen is a gift of human intention. Children who come home from school, open the door, and find the house full of the delicious scent of gingerbread just out of the oven know that a parent has made it for them as an act of love out of a desire to give them pleasure and nourishment.

It is not so in a garden. Some odors there please us, some we are indifferent to, and others repel us, but whether human beings like or dislike the way a particular plant smells is perfectly irrelevant, botanically speaking. When we welcome a sweet or spicy odor or turn away in revulsion from an unpleasant one, we are mere eavesdroppers on the olfactory messages sent by plants to their pollinators or their predators. But the conversation takes place in a language with a grammar and vocabulary we do not know, a chemical language that uses molecules instead of words. Plants speak this language, and the appropriate insects understand it precisely. We are latecomers to an ancient colloquy that has been going on since the first angiosperms, or flowering plants, appeared on land

*A*mong woody plants, none exceeds the gardenia for its deep, heady, and utterly delectable perfume. The richness of its scent is matched by flowers of surpassingly beautiful form and a pure whiteness few others can rival. [PHOTO BY ALLEN LACY]

some 114 million years ago—113.4 million years before *Homo sapiens* emerged on the planet.

The sweet smell of a rose or a narcissus is an advertisement directed at bees, and it's a good thing for us that bees carry out the major work of pollination. Some plants rely on flies instead, luring them with nasty odors of rotting flesh and worse. Scent in flowers is part of the strategy of plants to reproduce themselves. We may say that we find the perfume of gardenias seductive, and it is— but what the gardenia is trying to seduce is an insect, not a two-legged mammal.

Pleasantly scented or malodorous leaves are a different matter altogether. They send chemical signals that say, "Touch me not, eat me not—or else." We may find some of these signals agreeable and others most unpleasant, but in either case the message is the same. Crushed spearmint or nasturtium leaves may entice us, but the scents they give off, cool and refreshing in the one case and agreeably sharp and peppery in the other, are meant not to entice but to repel. The function of the volatile oils we find so bracing and invigorating in the leaves of mint or holy basil is the same as those of the physical mechanisms and toxic oils that make us regret brushing against bull nettle or stumbling through poison ivy. It is a pure evolutionary accident that our olfactory systems are wired up to relish the smells of rosemary, dill, and thyme. Other creatures are not so obtuse: they get the intended message, loud and clear. From our very inability to recognize a plant's chemical signals comes our pleasure. It is entirely our good fortune that we find much of the olfactory language some plants use to address creatures other than ourselves pleasant, although we do not fathom the language itself.

I began by pointing not only to the sensual appeal of fragrance but also to its mysteriousness. The mystery shows up as soon as we try to talk about the topic of smell, as it pertains to gardens or anything else. The problem is not lack of knowledge. We can recognize hundreds of odors from the slightest sniff, but our language to describe them is extraordinarily limited. In comparison with sight and hearing, our available vocabulary about what the nostrils know is poverty-stricken. In the vocabulary of the perceptual world of the eye, things *shimmer, glitter, gleam, fade, grow dim.* They are *crimson, scarlet, rose, mauve, purple, taupe, celadon.* They are *immense* or *tiny, slender* or *wide, gross* or *delicate.* It's the same with the world of the ear. Things *hiss, crackle, roar, whisper, murmur, rustle, tinkle.* By comparison, the language of odor is sparse and meager. Either we speak in rough, only approximate metaphors, saying that one odor is similar to another (itself not precisely captured in words), or we talk about the effects particular odors have upon us. Thus, the leaves of one plant smell like curry powder, those of another like pineapple, so we call the first "curry plant" and the second "pineapple sage"; thus, gardenias have a delightful odor, and the flowers of many members of the Aroid family are revolting.

Our experience of smell—whether it be the sweet scent of jasmines, the sharp tang of lemon peel, or the ugly stench of rotting garbage—is rich, but our ability to express this richness is severely limited. We are almost mute; we can speak only haltingly, and there is a reason. Smell is virtually preverbal. Molecular neurobiologists (who have achieved thus far only rudimentary understanding of the phenomena of olfaction and the closely related sense of gustation)

*P*erhaps the most hauntingly fragrant of the tropical angels' trumpets, Brugmansia versicolor *owes its species name to its rapid alterations of color. When the flowers open in the early evening, they are creamy white. Within minutes, they change to blush pink, as seen here. When they greet the morning, they are deep salmon. Their scent vanishes by day, but at night the plant's advertisement of itself to its nocturnal pollinators is almost palpable.*

explain that the sense of smell is the oldest of the sensory systems, viewed from the standpoint of evolution. All multicellular organisms—and even some single-cell organisms—possess exquisitely sensitive chemosensory systems that are essential to their survival in often unfriendly chemical environments. Smell differs from the visual and auditory systems in that it responds directly to the volatile molecules that stimulate it. In humans and other mammals, the other senses translate their stimuli—basically, vibrations in the air—into nerve impulses that travel to the higher centers of the brain. Smell, however, testifies almost directly to the oldest part of the brain, to what is sometimes called the reptilian brain.

From the meagerness of our ability to describe our olfactory world, it does not follow that our sense of smell is not acute: the fact is that an average human being can detect almost infinitesimal amounts of the ethyl mercaptan that is added to natural gas (which lacks odor) to alert us to its presence in the air we breathe. Nor does it follow that smell is an unimportant sense. Our nose warns us of danger when we catch a whiff of smoke or food that has gone bad. Someone who has lost the ability to smell—someone who is anosmic—is at risk from dangers the rest of us do not face. A strange, unfamiliar odor puts us immediately on guard, even as a pleasant and familiar one—bread baking in the oven or the perfume of wisteria from some distant corner of the garden—gives us a sense of safety.

Fragrance makes us feel at home in our gardens, and our gardens make us truly at home in the world.

Regal lilies are among the glories of the June garden—transcendently beautiful and with a heavy sweet fragrance that pervades the warm summer air.

CHAPTER 3

Tasting the Garden

Of all the senses, taste is the most intimately involved with the objects it perceives, because when we taste something we are generally about to eat it, to incorporate it in our bodies. If the taste is okay, we eat. If the taste is not okay, we are warned to go no further.

The experience of taste seems enormously rich and varied. Without looking, we can tell the differences between the tastes of lemons and limes, portabellos and shiitake. But the tongue is a great deceiver. Able to distinguish among a mere four basic tastes—sweet, sour, salty, and bitter—it takes credit for the much more sophisticated powers of discrimination possessed by the nose. When we say we "taste" something, be it garlic-roasted potatoes or a simple salad with oil and vinegar, the nose has done the real work, as the odors of what we are about to consume rise high into our nostrils.

When we taste and eat, what we are tasting and eating comes down to vegetation, sooner or later. If sooner, we eat a plant or a part of a plant directly: the leaves of collard greens, lettuce, and spinach; the flower buds of broccoli and cauliflower; the seeds and seed pods of okra and snow peas; the roots of radishes and carrots; the tubers of potatoes; the fruits of tomatoes, plums, and

LEFT: *Rosalind Creasy, a leading proponent of landscaping with edible plants, designed this attractive vegetable garden for Mudd's, a restaurant near Berkeley, California.*

oranges. If later, we feed on other creatures that nourished themselves on vegetation, like the steer that browsed on fresh green grass and dried hay and grain.

Plants are the original chemists. Their sophistication makes DuPont and Monsanto look like little kids with chemistry sets. A great many plants are highly toxic to human beings (and other animals as well) if ingested. Aconites, castor beans, daffodils, English ivy, foxgloves, and oleanders are only the beginning of a catalog of plants entirely poisonous or poisonous in part that would take many pages to list. Some plants have edible parts and toxic ones, too. Tomatoes and potatoes, both in the Nightshade family, have poisonous foliage, but we can safely eat the fruits of a tomato and the tubers of a potato. The red parts of rhubarb stems are safe to eat if they are boiled, but the green parts contain irritating toxic oxylates, and the leaves can be lethal. Even if a plant is not actually toxic it is unlikely, by strict percentage, to be palatable. Every time we sit down to dinner, we should say a little prayer of thanks to our supposedly primitive human ancestors. In the farthest reaches of our prehistoric times as a species they did a commendable job of working out what was okay to eat and what was not. There must have been many martyrs along the way.

Most gardeners manage to grow at least a few plants destined for their kitchens and their dining tables. They find room for three or four tomato plants in an odd corner. They tuck a few herbs—basil, chives, and parsley, minimally—into the front of their herbaceous border or grow them in pots on deck or patio.

For some, perhaps most, American gardeners, a garden's primary use is to raise food. For them, ornamental plants are strictly secondary, or merely companion plants for vegetables—e.g., marigolds to help check harmful nematodes and soil pathogens. They devote most of the sunny spots in their personal piece of real estate to a vegetable patch. Its size determines what they grow. If it is small and limited, they will surely grow tomatoes, peppers both hot and sweet, squash, lettuce, and perhaps a row each of beans, beets, carrots, and scallions, all for table consumption during high summer and early fall. If it is larger, they will grow leeks, potatoes and yams, sweet corn, melons, and pumpkins. Their herb gardens will enlarge to embrace lovage, marjoram, rosemary, thyme, and other aromatic plants. They will produce more than they and their families can eat during the growing season, so they will freeze or can the remainder for the rest of the year. If their space verges on immensity they will have bramble patches and orchards as well, so they can feast themselves on homegrown raspberries and dewberries, peaches, apples, figs, gooseberries, and other sweet-tasting gifts of the bounty of nature.

Some of us don't have vegetable patches, perhaps because our gardens are too shady, but it's easy to understand the appeal of raising as much food as possible on your own home ground. It's an extremely attractive endeavor. The food is fresh. The vegetables and fruits grown there have been selected for flavor, not shippability. If pesticides have been used, the gardener knows which ones, how much, and when.

Truly adventurous vegetable gardeners explore a world far beyond what they could find as easily at their local grocery stores as grow themselves. They grow Asian greens—pe-tsai, choy sum, mizuna—for salads and as potherbs. They try arugula, dandelions, chicory, corn salad, and orach. They add flowers to their gardens—calendulas, clove pinks, primroses, nasturtiums, and violets. But they use the blossoms as edible garnishes for their dining tables. (They agree with Bernard M'Mahon, the author of the first truly American garden book, *The American Gardener's Calendar* [11th Edition, 1857], that the nasturtium is "very deserving of cultivation. . . . The green berries of this plant make one of the nicest pickles that can be imagined; in the estimation of many, they are superior to capers.") They join the Seed Savers Exchange and do their part to keep heirloom vegetables like Jenny Lind melons and Turkey Craw pole beans from passing into oblivion. If they are truly sophisticated, they resolutely refuse to apologize to anyone for raising vegetables instead of the herbaceous perennials that have been in vogue in recent decades. They may call their garden a "potager" and point out proudly that Rosemary Verey has just such a kitchen garden at Barnsley House—and also occasionally designs them for others, including wealthy American expatriates living in France.

Such gardeners follow in the oldest traditions of horticulture, for ornamental gardening arrived eons after human beings began to garden to grow their food. A purely ornamental garden, one that supplies nothing to the dining table, is largely a creation of the twentieth century, its systems of transportation and distribution, its high degree of specialization, and its rigid control of the natural

Although the stuff of salads and sandwiches, a buttery head of lettuce at its peak of freshness pleases the eye, not just the palate.

order through F$_1$ hybrids and pesticides. To read books on gardening of the nineteenth century is to enter a lost world in which if people wanted strawberries they had to plant them, enjoy them during their brief season, and then settle for strawberry preserves the rest of the year. In world history, it is strictly an aberration of the prosperous Western countries at the dawning of the third millennium that the affluent among their citizens can eat strawberries—or tomatoes—365 days a year without troubling their heads over whether they grew in California, Chile, Israel, or just down the road. It's convenient—and sometimes the strawberries taste really good (seldom the tomatoes)—but it's also scary.

Not knowing where your food comes from is a primary form of alienation. And most Americans don't really know where their food comes from. In place of the small farms on which a large percentage of our forebears lived two or three generations ago, we have agribusiness. Food, we wrongly believe, just comes from grocery stores. Few of us have ever killed and drawn a chicken, for chickens come to us in shrink-wrap, courtesy of Perdue or Tyson. We have come to expect fresh peaches all year round almost as a birthright. It follows from this invisibility of the structures on which our lives depend that individuals, for the most part, have lost the knowledge to sustain themselves in the event of even the slightest failure in these systems.

There is an inherent aesthetic of order and discipline in a well-made kitchen garden. American gardeners, except for those smitten by the French intensive system of raising several kinds of vegetables in square patches, usually in raised beds or planters, lay out their kitchen gardens in rows, which shows sound practical wisdom. Rows make it easy to sow seed, to cultivate and weed, and to harvest, for the plants are at all times accessible. Form thus follows function—a twentieth-century notion in architecture, but an ancient one in domestic agriculture. Between the plants in their rows, the clean, cultivated earth shows—a pleasing reminder that we, like they, are rooted in soil, that humanity is akin to humus, in both etymology and truth.

Those of us whose vegetables come from the grocery store eat generically, but kitchen gardeners don't. We buy tomatoes, but they're just tomatoes. We don't know whether they are Rutgers, Champion, or Better Boy, and we thus cannot sharpen our senses by making comparisons, by detecting subtle differences of nuance between a First Lady and a Bonny Best. Kitchen gardeners can experiment. In a single year, they can try five different kinds of tomatoes—say,

Clad in golden down, peaches burst with juicy, opulent sweetness at summer's height, spurred on to delectable goodness by the heat of the July sun.

Although our modern system of food distribution assures that we can eat tomatoes all year round, they have their proper zest and tang only in late summer after ripening on the vine.

Brandywine, Celebrity, German Johnson, Hillbilly, and Mortgage Lifter. They can make minute comparative judgments about their quality, and they may decide that an old strain that is susceptible to cracking or catpacing (distinct disadvantages in a tomato grown to sell) nevertheless is superior to something better looking, because it tastes better in a salad or a soup, or eaten out of hand. At the end of one year, they may say, "Next year I'll surely grow this one, but I won't grow that one—I'll try something else instead." A kitchen garden exercises and may delight all the senses, including vision. (The congenitally sloppy as well as the relentlessly tidy delight in those rows, such evidences of order!)

All gardeners are, and must be, tuned in to the days and the seasons, but kitchen gardeners are exceptionally so. Ornamental plants may survive drought or excessive moisture, to return another season for a new start. But the vegetable garden exists under the old agrarian rhythm of seedtime and harvest, and harvest is the fulfillment.

The lives of kitchen gardeners have a social and communal dimension. What they plant is grown for consumption by other people—family, friends, and neighbors. Food raised for family and friends is shared at the table—and please note that although few nongardeners may appreciate your triumph in getting a difficult ornamental plant to flourish against all odds (for example, the Himalayan blue poppy, *Meconopsis betonicifolia,* in Vermont), everyone knows when they have just bitten into the luscious flesh of a perfect tomato.

Perhaps I romanticize the lives of kitchen gardeners, which is easy to do for someone who observes from afar something he used to do but does no longer. But this I know: by the sweat of their brows they are in touch with what is real and what is crucial in our own history. They raise domesticated plants for food.

The rest of us are hunters, foragers, and gatherers, but we hunt and gather at Safeway and Acme.

In *The Complete Book of Edible Landscaping* (1982), the California landscape architect Rosalind Creasy came forward with the sensible idea that by planting edible plants with attractive ornamental qualities instead of things like euonymus and yew, we could add the extra dimensions of taste and nutrition to our suburban yards and gardens. This idea isn't really new, for it revives what was an established American point of view in the nineteenth century. A. J. Downing's 1,098-page treatise, *The Fruits and Fruit Trees of America, or The Culture, Propagation, and Management, in the Garden and Orchard, of Fruit Trees Generally; with Descriptions of All the Finest Varieties of Fruit, Native and Foreign, Cultivated in This Country* (1845)—a title to reckon with!—rests on the assumption that most citizens will raise at least some of the fruits they eat. "In one part or another of the Union," Downing wrote, "every man may, literally, sit under his own vine and fig tree."

Judging from the way our garden centers fill up every spring with carpet junipers, forsythias, and Japanese flowering cherry trees, Creasy's argument has not made the headway it deserves, even though her book was well received. The idea of edible landscaping, however, still makes much good sense, especially as regards small fruits (with the possible exception of brambles, which have highly territorial ambitions, also prickles). Our native burning bush (*Euonymus elatus*) may be stunning for its glowing red foliage in the fall and its peculiarly winged stems, but highbush and lowbush blueberries (*Vaccinium corymbosum*

In the South, where they grow to the utmost perfection because summers are long and hot, the traditional time for eating watermelons lies between July 4 and Labor Day. No other fruit of the earth is quite so colorful, so fragrant, so juicy, or so welcome a gift to the taste buds and the soul.

and *V. angustifolium*), also native, are attractive in every season, given the acidic soil they prefer. They are among our most beautiful shrubs in late winter, when their stems assume tints of cerise and gold. Their fruits in summer, a strange shade of blue with a pewtery dusting or bloom, are handsome, although the taste is their main attraction. A couple of blueberry bushes may not produce much of a crop, of course, but it's still a pleasant thought that you grew the berries in your morning bowl of corn flakes and in the muffins hot right out of the oven.

There's not a whole lot of difference between the taste of a handful of blueberries right from the bush and that of a pint box from the grocer's, but figs are another matter entirely. Ripe figs don't travel well at all, and when they turn up at the produce counter they most likely have been picked green. Nothing on earth quite beats a fig at its peak of ripeness, eaten from the hand and still warm from the sun. Of course, fig trees take some trouble to grow where winters are severe, requiring wrapping with burlap, bending the branches to the ground and covering them with protective earth, or bringing them inside in containers to a cool basement—but fresh, ripe figs in summer repay the effort.

Kiwi vines also produce deliciously tart and astringent fruit. The Chinese kiwi, *Actinidia deliciosa* (which has nothing to do with New Zealand and its flightless birds), is not winter hardy in most of the United States, so we must resort to the grocery store for its large brown fuzzy egg-shaped fruits. But another species, *Actinidia arguta,* is hardy to Zone 4. Its green fruits are the size of grapes and have smooth, not downy, skin. Their texture is custardy, their taste both sharp and sweet. It's a handsome, highly ornamental, quick-growing vine that's ideal for covering a pergola. The fruits in the autumn are an added dividend.

Half hidden by their luxuriant foliage, clusters of ripening grapes hold within them the promise of harvest as autumn arrives.

The finest gustatory pleasure any garden can offer is ripe gooseberries, but finding truly good cultivars isn't easy. In the matter of gooseberries, home gardeners in Great Britain and Europe have it all over us, for a huge variety of cultivars adapted to their climate are sold there: red ones and purplish wine ones and green ones and golden ones and white ones; gooseberries for tarts, for jams, for plucking right off the prickly bushes and eating out of hand. Their flavors range from sweet to tart, with overtones of honey and lime. Reading Downing's *The Fruits and Fruit Trees of America* on gooseberries is both tantalizing and frustrating. He wrote that in 1845 over 149 named varieties were grown in England, especially in the vicinity of Lancashire, where weavers took special interest in raising and hybridizing them because they were easily grown in the small confines of a dooryard garden and were delicious in vast disproportion to the care they required and the space they occupied. Downing pointed out that some English gooseberries don't take well to the American climate, but he also described five cultivars—'Downing', 'Hobb's Seedling', 'Mountain Seedling', 'Pale Red', and 'Smith's Improved'—that were bred here, grew vigorously, and produced fruit that he rated as very good to excellent. None is available today. Virtually the only gooseberry that is easily found is 'Pixwell', which is hardly worth growing, as the fruits are small and insipid. For gooseberries that approach what gooseberries should be, superior cultivars such as 'Catherina', 'Glenndale', and 'Welcome' must be sought out at specialized nurseries.

It is hard to understand why every home garden in areas where peaches are hardy doesn't have at least one peach tree. No tree has lovelier blossoms in spring, and the dividend of fresh fruit in midsummer is no trifling thing. Ripe peaches don't travel well, and peaches that have ripened after picking lose much of their flavor and juiciness. There is nothing so fragrant, luscious, sweet, and delicious as a white-fleshed peach, and it never turns up in grocery stores—the fruit turns brown and spoils if you look at it hard.

A stroll around a garden, even if it's a garden that gives short shrift to fruits and vegetables, may still offer treats for casual nibbling. I enjoy munching on the leaves of chives, and of course I sip honeysuckle nectar whenever I can. The shining red berries of the creeping native shrub wintergreen (*Gaultheria procumbens*) have a fresh sharp spice, like wintergreen Life Savers—again no surprise. Nasturtium leaves and flowers are pleasantly peppery, like cress. I like to pick a stem of sweet goldenrod (*Solidago odora*) and savor its taste of anise. Sorrel has a lemony flavor, and its leaves are splendid in soup, as are those of lovage. I also enjoy the surprising leaves of the strange herb *Lippia dulcis,* which to the tongue is even sweeter than sugar; the Aztecs used it as a staple sweetener. The tender Paraguayan herb *Stevia rebudiana* is even sweeter—300 times as sweet as table sugar. Purslane may be considered a weed by some, but it is pleasantly spicy and agreeably crunchy.

As I wander through my garden, nibbling and munching, I am reminded of another sensual pleasure of tasting in a garden. What could be closer to paradise than to sit under a bower of vines on a hot July day, with bread and cheese and prosciutto, a slice of melon, and a tall glass of iced tea with mint?

*P*umpkins, seen here in some colors besides the usual orange of Halloween jack-o'-lanterns, are the final crop of the growing season, one that enriches our tables with soups and pies throughout winter.

CHAPTER 4

Listening to Gardens

No one perhaps has ever written a history of hearing, but it certainly has one. Just in our own waning century, human beings have done two extraordinary things: we have expanded the natural range of hearing, through radio and then through television, and we have managed to make sound more enduring by recording it. The political process is no longer limited by the inability of people to speak and listen to one another beyond a short distance. Few people ever heard the voices of Jefferson or Napoleon, but most of us today easily recognize those of FDR, JFK, and Elizabeth II.

Some important things about hearing, however, remain constant. One of them is that there is a difference between the sounds of the public world and those of the private world of the household. And whether we are talking about ancient Athens or Rome or contemporary life, the public world is far noisier than the private world.

The public world is now enormously noisier than it once was: decibel levels have increased almost exponentially in the last 100 to 150 years. Our ears are assaulted by a host of sounds our great-great-grandparents never knew nor dreamed of. Gasoline-powered engines contribute to the din. So do the sirens of ambulances, fire trucks, and police cars. Burglar alarms go off in the neighborhood. Garbage collection adds to the racket. Boom boxes enable unmannered, inconsiderate youths to inflict their musical tastes on unwilling listeners, and somewhat older adolescents drive cars rigged with sound systems so loud and powerful that they throb, vibrate, and pulsate like the mating calls of elephants. Electric guitars and a newer generation of electronic instruments rev up the volume to the threshold of pain and beyond. We live amid clatter and roar—harsh, angry, unforgiving sounds at ear-shattering decibel levels.

The public world, moreover, increasingly intrudes on the private world. Television brings us endless arguments to buy this or that, to support this political party and reject another one, to believe that happiness may come from changing brands of underarm deodorant. The telephone rings at dinnertime, and someone we don't know implores us to get a new credit card, change brokers, redo our kitchen cabinets, or give another $100 to support the good works of some nonprofit organization

We need some retreat and refuge from the din of the public world, a place to escape from the intrusions on our privacy, some haven where we can hear ourselves think. Gardeners are lucky souls, for we have just such a place. Few of us, of course, can escape entirely from the din of the public world, for few of us have gardens that are sufficiently remote from the street to do the trick. But in a garden, these sounds are at least muffled. Furthermore, when we are occupied with a repetitive task like pulling weeds or when we are absorbed with wonder over some new flower that has just come into bloom, we pay less attention to the sounds that come from outside the garden.

The characteristic sounds of a garden have changed very little in the last 100 years—or 700, for that matter—and some of the new sounds that have come along are not unpleasant. I don't think anyone could object to the soft, rhythmic susurration of the automatic sprinkler system. In "Knoxville: Summer, 1915," the prologue to *A Death in the Family* (1957), James Agee waxed lyrical on the remembered sound of the fathers in his neighborhood performing the evening rite of sprinkling their lawns, adjusting the nozzles of their hoses to produce a spray described as a "compromise between distance and tenderness," which filled the air with the sound of a great nocturnal chorus. Once heard, it was a sound never to be forgotten. Lawn mowers, of course, are a comparatively new sound in gardens, the push mower having been invented by Edmund Budding in England in the 1840s. I find the low, whispering whir a delicious sound, one that triggers childhood memories of summer Saturdays when my father mowed the lawn. Power mowers are more recent inventions, to be sure, as are electric or gasoline-powered shredders and leaf blowers, all of which are loud and noisy contraptions. Fortunately, their work is quickly done, and when it is accomplished quiet returns to the garden.

A garden's quietude does not mean the absence of sound. Gardens make their own music. Much of it is barely above the threshold of conscious perception. It does not insistently make itself be heard: it must be listened to, attended to with a receptive ear.

In *Home and Garden* (1900), Gertrude Jekyll wrote that her increasing weakness of vision was made up for by extraordinarily keen hearing. If she heard a faint rustling in dry leaves, she could determine by her ear alone whether it was a mouse, a lizard, or a snake. She could identify birds overhead by the sound of their flight, even if their calls were silent. In a wind, she could determine whether a tree was a birch, oak, chestnut, fir, or poplar by the rustling of its leaves. "The voice of Oak leaves," she wrote, "is . . . rather high-pitched, though lower than that of Birch. Chestnut leaves in a mild breeze sound much more deliberate; a sort of slow slither. Nearly all trees in gentle wind have a pleasant sound, but I confess to a distinct dislike to the noise of all Poplars; feeling it to be painfully fussy, unrestful, and disturbing." Miss Jekyll continues, saying that Scotch firs have a "soothing and delightful" murmur, but the strangest-sounding foliage belongs to the Virginia allspice, *Calycanthus floridus,* "whose leaves are of so dry and harsh a quality that they seem to grate and clash as they come together."

I have listened to the leaves of my own Virginia allspice. I detect no grate or clash, but there is no reason to doubt Miss Jekyll's claim to such remarkable auditory acuity, for she was highly observant. Some of the trees in my garden do have distinctive voices in the breeze, even if I probably would not be able to identify them blindfolded. A fifty-foot dawn redwood (*Metasequoia glyptostroboides*) rustles almost constantly, in tremulous motion from top to bottom at the air's faintest movement, its leaves whispering like little children telling secrets. A weeping mulberry, *Morus alba* 'Pendula', which is utterly lovely in every season, makes exquisite music when in full leaf. Its long, hanging stems catch the slightest breeze, swishing back and forth with a sound somewhere between a murmur and a sigh.

Gertrude Jekyll was far from being the first English writer to dwell on the sensual pleasure of listening to rustling leaves. In *A Treatise on Fruit Trees* (1653), Ralph Austen wrote that a garden orchard gave two gifts to the ear. One was "the sweet notes and tunes of singing Birds," the other "hearing the slow motion of Boughes and Leaves . . . which will easily induce a sweet and pleasant sleep in sommer time (if a man be dispos'd) in some close coole Arbor or shady seat."

Ornamental grasses are a garden's playthings of the wind. The sounds they make vary with the seasons. When their foliage has matured in late summer and moves with the wind, it makes a soft, rippling noise, like little waves washing up on a lakeshore. In flower, their plumes make a swishing sound. Later in the year, when the seeds have ripened, their rustle is dry and rasping. The various ornamental grasses have enjoyed a great and growing popularity over the last decade for many good reasons, but the sound and movement they bring to a garden are sufficient grounds for planting them.

Bamboos have a beauty all their own, including beauty to the ear. The leaves, like those of the dawn redwood, whisper constantly. A sudden strong burst of wind can make their sturdy stems clatter against one another like a percussive instrument. After reading the words of the Chinese poet Bo Ju'yi: about loving to lie near a window to hear the sound of the autumn wind in bamboo

This pair of whimsical clay masks in the garden of Chris Rosmini in Californa caters to the ear. One burbles continuously beneath the surface of a small pond; when a breeze stirs, the other whispers with the delicate, swishing murmur of bamboo leaves in the wind.

In Provence, this pleasant garden seat lies near ornamental grasses that please the ear with their agreeable soft music in the slightest breeze.

branches, Elizabeth Lawrence planted an evergreen species near her own house in Charlotte. "All winter the green leaves rustle outside my window," she wrote, "and the low winter sun sends slender shadows into the room."

The window of my study, kept closed on hot, humid summer days for the sweet relief of air-conditioning, looks out on our back garden, but the canopy of a quince tree blocks my view of the ground. I see but do not hear the foliage rustling. Finally the invitation to leave the house and go into the garden cannot be resisted. I sit beneath the pergola, listening to the lyrical sounds the garden makes. A dimension has been restored to experience.

With autumn arrives the seasonal pleasure of falling leaves. As the leaves begin to build up, I like to shuffle through them, hearing their dry rustle underfoot, putting off as long as possible that final chore of the gardening year—raking the leaves and hauling them to the compost heap. The scratch of the rake is another pleasant sound, as are the voices of my neighbors, come outdoors to perform the same chore on their own home grounds.

The hospitality that a garden offers to wildlife is directly proportionate to the quantity and diversity of its vegetation. A brand-new house fresh from the developer's hand, with a green lawn out front and back, foundation plants of juvenile yews and junipers set out symmetrically along its front, and concrete driveway and sidewalks, can support only a meager population of animal life. The heavy doses of pesticides too often used unthinkingly by people who believe that their yards should be rigidly controlled further reduce this population.

But when front yards and back yards are turned into gardens, the welcome mat is out. We can build our own field of dreams, telling ourselves, correctly, "Plant it—and they will come." A diversity of well-chosen shrubs and trees provides nesting sites for songbirds—and food as well, if forethought is given to woody plants with edible fruits and seed heads.

As a garden matures, its fauna swell in number. Songbirds find places to hide their nests and raise their young. In my garden there is the constant chatter of jays—often, it seems, in a duet with squirrels. Mockingbirds sing sweetly at dawn. The starlings that use our hollow maple as a condominium are nasty and raucous, but their young whistle in a strangely appealing way. Robins, cardinals, catbirds, purple finches, and sparrows add their own music. Mourning doves sit on the telephone wires above the sidewalk, addressing one another with low cooing sounds. Other birds, well outside the garden, join the chorus. Owls somewhere nearby hoot at dawn and dusk. Flocks of seagulls and other shorebirds pass overhead, loquacious and gossipy. Fall and spring are marked by the honking passage of V-shaped formations of migratory geese along the Atlantic flyway that lies directly overhead.

Listening to bird calls has its mysteries. They are clearly saying something to one another, but the language can almost never be translated into human language, with one exception: birds let the whole world know when a cat is on the prowl.

Birds are not the only creatures that turn a garden into a symphony for ears that know how to listen. Chipmunks are appealing little beings that scurry about their errands and dart in and out of hiding, chattering among themselves. As for squirrels, who would wish to live in a garden without a few on the premises? They have some annoying habits, like burying walnuts everywhere and then forgetting them. But their testy, scolding voices are lively and pointed, and I love to hear the noise they make when they turn daredevil and go aerial. When they chase one another through the branches of a paulownia tree in fall and winter, the seedpods clatter like castanets.

From spring onward, insects put in their word. Bumblebees and honeybees are constantly working the daylight hours, buzzing about us. As summer wears

If there's a cat prowling around a garden, birds will sound an alarm to let each other—and us—know all about it.

on, the sounds of grasshoppers and crickets fill the air. On hot July afternoons male katydids rasp out their brassy sexual song in a chorus that rises out of silence to a crescendo and then diminishes, while cicadas buzz their similar hymn of desire and availability from high in the trees.

In the public world, highways, shopping malls, and suburban developments carved out of woodlands have altered and often destroyed the natural habitats of birds and other wildlife. We have laid down hundreds of thousands of square miles of asphalt and concrete. We have clear-cut entire forests, altered land contours with steam shovels and bulldozers, destroyed vast prairie ecosystems, and filled wetlands, leaving ugly scars on the earth as testimony to progress and development. We have been careless about polluting chemicals, including pesticides that are harmful to wildlife. As private individuals, we can do very little about such environmental havoc, although we should of course try, lending our

*The buzz of bumblebees, as
seen here on a spectacularly
fringed blossom of* Inula
magnifica, *is part of
the music of a garden.*

shoulders and our checkbooks to anything that may bring a little more sanity
into the public world. But as gardeners, we can do a lot on the tiny plots of earth
where we live. We can plant to suit the needs of the birds and other wildlife that
find a haven and a habitat on our home ground, and we can understand that to
do so is a moral dictate, not a personal whim. We owe something to the creatures that inhabit our private world, because they unknowingly give us a precious pleasure. What satisfaction when suddenly there is a high-pitched whir
and a tiny, jeweled hummingbird appears briefly, hovering in midair, drinking
nectar from the flower of a trumpet vine or fuchsia and then darting out of
sight, in a disappearance as sudden and unpredictable as its appearance!

Using our ears to listen to the songs and other utterances of the wildlife in
our gardens opens us up to the natural order, connecting us with a small fraction of it.

Water, especially moving water, is cooling, and the mere sound of it
refreshes body and spirit. In the summer of 1955, while still in college, I lived
with a family in Guadalajara in the Mexican state of Jalisco, in a house with an
interior patio garden that centered on a stone fountain with a sparkling jet of
water that made lovely, crystalline music day and night.

Many years later, my family and I spent much of a sabbatical year in Spain
in a small house entirely surrounded by a lush garden shaded by fragrant euca-
lyptus trees and castor bean plants of heroic proportions. Water was everywhere, in many forms—lily pools and fishponds and a tiled pool for our sons to

splash in and play with toy boats, a terra-cotta wall plaque with a bas-relief lion dripping water from its mouth, and, somewhere in the distance, a pool with a water jet whose sound lulled us to sleep at night and woke us at dawn.

That year we also traveled, visiting gardens in Seville, Cordova, and, of course, Granada, where we made a pilgrimage to the most sensual and inspiring of all Spain's palace gardens, the Alhambra. I knew to expect water in this massive fortress high above Granada, for Washington Irving had written about it extensively in *The Alhambra* (1832). Irving lived in this Moorish palace, then dilapidated, in the 1820s, and his still highly readable book combines romantic legends of princesses and robbers in bygone times with keen observations on Islamic architecture and gardens. Here, Irving said, he found "everything to delight a southern voluptuary, fruits, flowers, fragrance, green arbors and myrtle hedges, delicate air, and gushing waters." A copious supply of water "brought from the mountains by old Moorish aqueducts," he noted, "circulates throughout the palace, supplying its baths and fish pools, sparkling in jets within the halls, or murmuring in channels along the marble pavements."

But I was really not prepared for the *experience* of water in the Alhambra, and in the Generalife above it. Water sits in long still pools, reflecting the delicate, jewel-like tracery and complex calligraphy of the arches on flanking colonnades. It bubbles up from basins of dark gray stone. In the Court of the Lions it pours from the mouths of twelve droll lions set round a font with a tall jet at its center, the lions facing outward to twelve points on the compass. At their feet the water collects in a polygonal trough, then flows in four directions the length and breadth of the open courtyard and beyond. The Generalife, originally a summer residence on much higher and breezier ground, is pure waterplay. Along both sides of a long, narrow rectangular pool, jets lift high their curving streams of sparkling water, filling the air with mist and spray, so cool that you have to catch your breath when stray drops fall on your cheeks.

I would not want to say that no one can have a garden worthy of the name if it has no water to be heard. But I will say that water always adds to the pleasures gardens yield, although jets and elaborate fountains are out of place in the small gardens most of us have nowadays.

Water does more than give the suggestion of coolness. It also cools the air. It is no accident that the styles of gardening that have used it most prominently

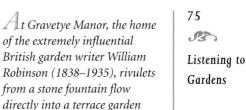

*At Gravetye Manor, the home
of the extremely influential
British garden writer William
Robinson (1838–1935), rivulets
from a stone fountain flow
directly into a terrace garden
where bees buzz industriously
among flowers of purple sage
and centranthus.*

have developed in places with torrid summer climates, like Persia and Andalusia. By any reckoning, the summer months in Charleston, South Carolina, are best described as beastly. The gardens of the city's historic district take perhaps greater advantage of water than gardens anywhere else in America. Scarcely a garden is to be found there without its pool and tiny fountain, without the cooling sounds of water trickling, gushing, or splashing.

When it rains, I love the first sounds of raindrops hitting the leaves of the old maple tree in the middle of the back garden. I rejoice in the rumble of thunder in the far distance, and my adrenaline rises if the storm bursts full upon us. As the sudden strong wind bends the branches of trees, sets leaves into furious tremor, and hurls a pot of hibiscus from the deck to the lawn, we dash inside to close windows and batten things down. If there's lightning nearby, and the

A small ceramic fountain lends its trickling sound to David Rawls's walled patio garden in Charleston, South Carolina.

thunder is no longer a rumble but a series of crashing explosions, there comes the slightly perverse joy the Germans call Schadenfreude—the delight in danger and in the potentially destructive forces of nature.

No garden should be without at least one set of wind chimes, but there are wind chimes and there are wind chimes. Listen before buying is a sound rule. Ours have six highly polished stainless steel tubes sweetly tuned to ring in random harmony in the slightest breeze as they swing into one another or against their central wooden clapper. One so quickly gets used to wind chimes that their music goes almost unnoticed, but when a windstorm approaches their furious silvery pealing sounds a lovely and unmistakable alarm.

Then there are the human voices. The telephone rings inside the house and a moment later I hear Hella answering. The sounds of children splashing, diving into the water, and laughing among themselves at our neighbor's swimming pool on warm weekends are cheering and friendly. A couple on an evening stroll passes by on our sidewalk, their voices audible but their words indecipherable. Working in the depths of a perennial bed, I hear a car pull into the driveway, a door open, and one of my grandchildren calling out, "Opi, where are you? I'm in your garden."

And there's music. The sound of Samuel Ramey singing "Ombra mai fù" pours through the French doors to the deck from the living room, where the CD player dwells. Then Hella changes the CD, and the bright blare of trumpets announces the opening bars of Bach's Magnificat in D, surging toward the entrance of the chorus: "Magnificat anima mea Dominum." For a moment I'm a boy alto in Texas again, and then I think enviously about the garden of my

In Patti McGee's enclosed garden in Charleston, South Carolina, a glass ball floats serenely in a reflective pool where a tiny fountain off to one side sounds like raindrops beginning to fall at the onset of a summer storm.

friend Patti in Charleston, right across from St. Stephen's Episcopal Church. Every Sunday she can hear the choir and congregation chanting the office of morning prayer.

On rare occasions, silence itself can be listened to. Suddenly there is no street traffic, no breeze is stirring, no leaves rustle, birds have forgotten to sing. Calm descends on the little world of the garden for one brief moment: I hear only the beating of my heart. Or snow begins falling on a windless day, cloaking the world in white, muffling its every familiar and accustomed sound.

Throughout the year, our garden is speechless. But it nevertheless says things to us—and we have learned to listen.

CHAPTER 5

The Education of the Eye

Gardening is in large measure a phenomenon of attention. Something grabs us, calling on us to pay heed, and we cannot resist. It may be just one plant. We come around the corner in a friend's or relative's garden one drizzly morning, encounter a gardenia bush in full bloom, its dazzling white flowers and glossy dark green foliage spangled with raindrops, the air around us filled with delicious, unforgettable perfume, and we know—we must have gardenias in our lives from then on, and a garden to grow them in. Sometimes it's one particular kind of plant that seizes our attention, permanently and to the exclusion of anything else. We become fervent lovers of roses, devotees of daylilies, members of the hosta or dahlia tribe, unable to see any other plants than the object of our affection. We may remain faithful in our partisanship ever thereafter, or we may change our affections, in the horticultural equivalent of serial monogamy. There is no rule about when any of this happens. Someone may fall in love with bearded irises at the age of eight (thus it happened with me), or suddenly discover at fifty that there's a world of orchids and their enthusiasts, a world that simply must be entered and explored without delay. Gardening is a love affair. All gardeners have their stories. Their passions have their histories, and no two histories are exactly the same.

Nevertheless, there is a logical progression in the lives of many, if not all, gardeners, particularly as regards the stages in their visual appreciation of gardens. Each stage differs from the preceding in the object of its attention.

At the initial stage it is flowers at their very height of bloom that attract us. What attracts us to flowers is their colors; their names are virtually irrelevant. What is crucial is color as a primary sensation—or better, colors, in the plural. This point is always immediately evident when small children come to visit our garden. They respond eagerly to the things I point out to them, the feel, the smell, and the taste of various plants, and once they have been taught these things they keep going back to them. It's different with color. Color speaks to them directly. Like honeybees, they find the flowers in a garden on their own. A johnny-jump-up or dandelion blossom is quite enough to win their attention. It's almost certain that color is the lure.

Frances Hodgson Burnett's classic *Secret Garden* (1911)—a book that more than any other I can think of has convinced many a child that the one essential thing to do on growing up is to become a gardener—buttresses my conviction that for a child color is the Pied Piper of the garden. At the novel's climactic moment, when Mary and Dickon first take their friend Colin to the abandoned garden they have brought back to life—even as they have helped him move from the life of an invalid to the promise of health—Colin opens his eyes in delight at what he sees.

> And over walls and earth and trees and swinging sprays and
> tendrils the fair green veil of tender little leaves had crept, and
> in the grass under the trees and the grey urns in the alcoves and
> here and there everywhere were touches or splashes of gold and
> purple and white and the trees were showing pink and snow
> above his head—

Colin, to be sure, also pays heed to the other sensual appeals of this magical garden:

> and there were flutterings of wings and faint sweet pipes and
> humming and scents and scents. And the sun fell warm upon
> his face.

At this point, his friends see how his first sight of the garden has transformed him, how color has worked its healing magic on him.

And in wonder Mary and Dickon stood and stared at him. He looked so strange and different because a pink glow of colour had actually crept over him—ivory face and neck and hands and all.

'I shall get well! I shall get well!' he cried out. 'Mary! Dickon! I shall get well! And I shall live for ever and ever and ever!'

If color is the main attraction of flowers, it stands to reason that the more colors there are, the better. I recall that when I first learned—and we are talking a long time ago—that I could buy packets of seed, sow them, have the seeds come up and eventually bloom, it was the packets of seed in mixed colors that attracted me. Why spend thirty cents for six packets of zinnias in six different colors when I could spend five cents (I told you were are talking about a long time ago) for a packet that would produce zinnias in six different colors and a whole lot more?

Sowing seed was an anxious pursuit. First came the wait to see if anything would come up. It usually did. Then came the wait to see what color the flowers would be. Those of "rose moss" (the peculiar vernacular term in Texas for portulaca) were mostly magenta, but there were other colors, shades, and hues, almost everything but purple, true blue, and a genuine red. But the greatest fascination came from four o'clocks, because of their brilliant but peculiarly unstable colors. They didn't have to be planted from seed, for they sow themselves, and in the South, where they are as omnipresent as atmosphere, they return every year from their underground tubers.

Along with morning glories, portulaca, and moonflowers, four o'clocks marked the stages of a hot summer day. Heavenly Blue morning glories and portulaca were up and blooming at the first touch of the sun, but by noon they were gone—the morning glories limply hanging their aged faces in a terminal wilt, the portulaca petals turned to mush. Soon after my afternoon nap, however, the four o'clocks in my mother's garden would begin to wake up. When their sweetly fragrant, little flat trumpet flowers opened, I knew it wouldn't be long before I could hear the clink of ice in the kitchen as my mother made a big pitcher of iced tea with mint. After supper, the long tapering buds of the moonflowers would begin to unfurl, becoming great white saucers with a delicious

The four o'clock, or marvel of Peru (Mirabilis jalapa)*, was one of the first ornamental plants of the New World to create excitement in Europe, for its odd habit of producing flowers of several different colors on the same plant.* [PHOTO BY ALLEN LACY]

scent in the air of the fading day. Morning glories, portulaca, four o'clocks, and moonflowers: these gave the summer days of childhood their order and rhythm.

I was delighted by the play of color in the flowers of four o'clocks—the different colors of flowers on the same plant, the different colors in one blossom. A four o'clock plant could produce all pink flowers, all yellow ones, or all pale lilac. It could produce some of each. Or it could produce flowers that were half one color, half another. Or it could produce flowers of one, two, or three shades that were dotted and streaked with something else, in a delightfully capricious way. "You have to decide what you want to be when you grow up," my parents and grandparents had already warned me. I thought this was a very bad thing to look forward to. Four o'clocks offered an encouraging lesson: perhaps, when I grew up, I could be several things all at once. Its colors told me so.

In the life of the passionate gardener, the love of color for its own sake eventually becomes subordinate to other visual appeals, but it never entirely vanishes. Furthermore, it strikes me that for people who enjoy gardens without being personally interested in gardening as a pursuit, colorful flowers are the chief immediate appeal (at least at the level of conscious awareness: unconsciously they are as responsive to the intelligence and creativity that go into well-designed gardens as anyone else). Thus, many gardens open to the paying public rely heavily on floral displays that make extravagant and spectacular use of color. There is no better example of such a garden than Butchart Gardens, outside of Victoria, British Columbia. It is a huge tourist attraction that owes much of its popularity and fame to its success in pleasing the general public by its lavish display of bright colors.

Butchart is a feast for the eyes, absolutely awash with color from spring to the end of fall. Blessed with a fortunate climate, it enjoys a prolonged and gentle summer. Its main source of color is bedding annuals and tender perennials treated as annuals, all planted in large masses of a single kind almost everywhere you can look, except for the emerald green, exquisitely tended lawns. Calceolarias, celosias, fuchsias, impatiens, lobelias, marigolds, nicotianas, petunias, salpiglossis, tuberous begonias—at least fifty kinds of such plants are the mainstays of Butchart's flamboyant plantings.

On several visits to Butchart, I have eavesdropped quite a lot, particularly at the exit to the parking lot, trying to figure out what brought people here and whether they were satisfied at the end of their visit. It was easy to spot fairly sophisticated gardeners, for the words that emerged from their lips were things like "gaudy," "vulgar," and "floral overkill."

Most of the visitors who come to Butchart, however, don't seem to be horticulturally minded, and they leave very well pleased with what they have seen.

"Lovely, just lovely."

"Absolutely gorgeous. I never knew there were so many colors in the world."

People come to Butchart, it would seem, primarily to see "flowers," almost in a generic sense, the way some people go to the Grand Canyon to see "scenery," to a concert to hear "music," to an art museum to see "pictures and statues." This garden should be understood in terms of what it is. It must make its appeal to the largest possible number of people who have come for a brief

Butchart Gardens, outside of Victoria, British Columbia, pleases hundreds of thousands of visitors annually by its extremely colorful displays of massed bedding annuals.

*T*he pool in the enclosed courtyard outside the tea room at Butchart Gardens is surrounded by flamboyant wax begonias, with mixed annuals spilling out of window boxes atop the fences.

visit, possibly the only visit they will ever make. Behind-the-scenes maintenance is intense. Flowers are whisked into beds just as they come into bloom, and when they start to fade they are yanked out and replaced. Crews of workers constantly remove spent blossoms before they set seed. Visitors are never given a chance to feel that they've come a week too soon or a week too late. It is a garden that gives the strong impression of being for the present moment, for the *now*.

It doesn't take much thought to figure out that, in succeeding extremely well in its purpose of pleasing great numbers of mostly onetime visitors over a long season by giving them huge doses of floral color, this garden depends on vast technical knowledge and expertise—and on exquisitely exacting planning.

Such planning must encompass, first, the selection of plants, and, second, a precise schedule for growing them from seed, cuttings, or bulbs under rigidly controlled conditions of light, moisture, and temperature. Nothing can be left to accident. The same kind of planning is essential in the florist industry with Easter, except that florists have it easy: they need worry only about holidays (religious and secular) that occur once each year. Butchart has to put on the equivalent of Easter every day it's open to the public.

Love of colorful flowers is primal. The appeal of color is primal. It makes its first appearance in earliest childhood. It stays with us ever after, but it is still only a first step in the progress and further education of the eye.

Flowers may clamor to stake the first claim on our attention, although of course they are really playing to the insects and other pollinators that make plant reproduction possible. But blossoming is only one event in a plant's life history (and some plants—ferns, for example—do not flower but reproduce themselves by other mechanisms). Accordingly, the next stage in the education of the gardener's eye is a matter of attention to the nonfloral parts of plants, starting with the foliage that carries on the photosynthesis essential to a plant's life—and indeed to all other life.

Color also comes to the fore again in foliage, and not just in fall with its brilliant conflagration. We must start, obviously, with green. In its many tints and hues, green dominates in the leaves of plants, for it is the color of the chlorophyll on which all life depends. The very etymology of "green" teaches this lesson, for it derives from the same Old English root that also gives us "grow" and "grass." But green is certainly not the only pigment plants produce. Green should probably be the dominant color in any good garden, but it needs to be set off by contrasting colors. In time, most gardeners move beyond the kindergarten Crayola mentality that says if it's a leaf, then color it green.

The color of foliage other than green is an entirely different beast than floral color. Such adjectives as "blue" and "purple" have the same meaning in flowers that they have in paint stores and automobile showrooms. With foliage (except again for green) the names of colors should either be enclosed in quotation marks or have -ish tacked on. There may be fair agreement among gardeners that hostas like *Hosta sieboldiana* 'Elegans' have blue leaves, but it's really a bluish-grayish or glaucous shade. It's the blue of slate, not of sapphires. "Purple" more often than not is really maroon or chestnut—reddish-brown, in fact. These words denote tendencies, not actualities.

It makes sense to divide colored foliage into three groups: the dark colors (purples, reds, and blackish tones); the medium colors (blues and grays); and the light colors (yellows, golds, and chartreuses). Into a fourth category fall plants with leaves that are variegated with two or more colors. Because the effects of reflected sunlight upon each group differ, each has different uses in a garden.

Dark colors tone things down and give a sense of subdued calm. A number of useful annuals help create this feeling of repose—and some do double duty in the kitchen. Basil 'Dark Opal', ruby chard, and giant red mustard, an Asian potherb, all qualify for these purposes. In recent years, a great many new heucheras with brown-maroon to purplish foliage have been introduced since the importation in 1985 of the Palace Purple strain—which figures prominently in the ancestry of most of the more recent cultivars. A number of other fine perennials and also tender tropical or subtropical plants qualify as fitting into this general category, as do such woody plants as the purple-leafed redbud, *Cercis canadensis* 'Forest Pansy', and an especially fine cultivar of the purple smoke tree, *Cotinus coggygria* 'Royal Purple'.

Turning to the medium tones, gray and blue-gray or glaucous foliage is the great pacifier of gardens. Gray and related hues fight with no other color, but live in harmony with them all. They never shout or push forward for attention. Gray furthermore can separate warring colors from one another. The color has a peaceful neutrality of its own that suggests dignity and rest.

A garden with some age to it is likely to be a garden with an ample ration of grays and the related silvers and pewters. Woolly thyme will creep between flagstones or other paving materials in sunny walks. Perennial borders will long ago have welcomed gray-leaved plants like rose campion, silver sage, lamb's ears, and the better-behaved sorts of artemisias. If the garden is especially fortunate, it may have as its special treasure a specimen of *Pyrus salicifolia* 'Pendula', the weeping silver pear that Vita Sackville-West planted as the centerpiece of her famous white garden at Sissinghurst. It personifies grace and elegance.

Love for plants with foliage at the chartreuse-to-yellow-to-gold part of the spectrum comes slowly, but once established, it's a lifelong affair. There's a certain amount of prejudice to overcome—one must set aside the notion that yellowish leaves are a sign that something is amiss with a plant, some deficiency of nutrients or minerals perhaps, or maybe some horrible disease. A garden made up entirely of such plants would no doubt be jarring, the absence of unmistakable greens unsettling. (But possibly not. After all, Americans are in love with our woodlands in the autumn, when they are a furnace of flaming reds and oranges and incandescent yellows and golds, with no greens in sight except those of evergreen conifers.)

Plants with yellow or golden foliage, whether woody or herbaceous, add variety to a garden. If plants with dark foliage suggest repose and those with gray foliage create harmony where there would otherwise be conflicts of color, those with bright-colored leaves fairly shout for attention—golden common privet and the golden box honeysuckle, *Lonicera nitida* 'Baggeson's Gold', come to mind—and they pump color into dim nooks that would be drab without them.

Of all plants, those with variegated foliage have the closest association, except for food plants, with the human race. The reason is simple. Variegated plants almost entirely come into being as mutations among plants that originally were of a single color, generally green. The whites or yellows that originate in this way indicate a reduction in the amount of chlorophyll that would not allow these plants to survive in the wild, in competition with the stronger individuals from which they arose. Whether they are splashed with gold or white, striped with chartreuse or cream, or margined in light tones, they are nature's weaklings, and nature is still a matter of the survival of the fittest. The survival of variegated plants depends on human intervention.

Human intervention in their survival, of course, has as its prerequisite human notice. If there is any huge trend in American and European horticulture today, it's an extremely keen interest in variegated forms of plants whose foliage is generally green. Let such a plant—an eastern dogwood whose leaves are marked with blotches of gold, or a daylily whose foliage is edged in white—appear in the gardens of those who are attentive to such things, and it will instantly be set aside for anxious observation. More often than not, such muta-

The contrasting textures and colors of golden filipendula, variegated Solomon's seal, and a fern combine to form a pleasing and long-lasting garden picture.

Introduced in 1985 by Glasshouse Works, Canna × generalis 'Striata' has rapidly become one of the most sought after of all variegated plants. Here in the garden of Edward and Anna Crawford on Meeting Street in Charleston, South Carolina, it is superb with Salvia guaranitica.

tions are unstable. They disappear in the triumph of chlorophyll over aesthetics. (I have been disappointed on several occasions by such reversions. A bee balm with golden-edged leaves, a European wild ginger speckled with silver, a royal fern whose fronds were strongly banded in soft yellow, and a common *Hosta undulata* that was entirely creamy white instead of white and green—I put hope in all of them, wishing that they would prove stable, could be propagated by vegetative means, and go out into the gardening world as my special gift. But all were creatures of a single season, no more than two at best, and in the case of the hosta, three weeks, as it died in May after it appeared in April.)

Current interest in variegated plants is so fervent that there's little if any doubt that should a mutation appear in poison ivy that would, say, give it leaves with white margins or perhaps the gaudy combination of green, red, and yellow found in *Houttuynia cordata* 'Chameleon', it would rapidly travel from one coast to another through the informal but lively network that links American gardeners of the variegated avant-garde. It's less than certain that in every case a variegated form of a plant whose leaves are ordinarily green is really an improvement, rather than simply a novelty. But certain variegated plants are virtually indispensable in a well-made garden. It would be hard to go without the Japanese painted fern, *Athyrium nipponicum* 'Pictum', whose fronds are a toothsome combination of green, pewter, and raspberry, or without the variegated Solomon's seal, *Polygonatum odoratum* 'Variegatum', which bears pairs of fragrant, greenish white flowers beneath its white-edged leaves on gracefully arching stems. It would be hard to give up the yellow and green variegated form of *Canna × generalis* that at present goes around under three different names ('Striata', 'Pretoria', and 'Bengal Tiger'), for it is a highly dramatic accent plant that lends a tropical note to any landscape. And if some horticultural czar were to order us all to get rid of all our ornamental grasses but one, the choice would be easy, for the Japanese woodland grass *Hakonochloa macra* 'Aureola' is purely wonderful for its graceful foliage. Creamy yellow thinly striped in green, it grows in one direction, as if being raked by a stiff wind.

As for hostas—well, can there be any dispute over their being the truly indispensable herbaceous foliage plants? Most species and many cultivars are green, a good, solid, glossy deep green that bespeaks dignity and quiet calm, but the genus is given to sudden fits of mutation that send it exploring other parts

At Sheila Macqueen's Westwick Cottage in Hertfordshire, the golden foliage of Ribes sanguineum *contrasts splendidly with the blue-green foliage of* Hosta sieboldiana *'Elegans' and the variegated leaves of the popular hosta 'Frances Williams'. This combination of plants, which owes nothing to floral color, remains effective and attractive throughout the growing season.*

of the spectrum. The dark tones, the purples and reds and blacks, aren't found in hosta foliage yet, but maybe they will be: hostas are wont to throw up wonderful surprises, and already a few cultivars have appeared with reddish-purple leaf petioles. There are many good "blues," like 'Lovepat', 'Fragrant Blue', and *H. sieboldiana* 'Elegans'. No garden should be without 'Sum and Substance', a chartreuse-gold with leaves large enough to serve a luau on, or 'Sun Power', whose golden glow brings warmth to cool, dark corners. The variegated ones are superb, too. 'Frances Williams', an old cultivar with gold and green variegated leaves of considerable size on plants that bulk large in the shady border, pretty much started the craze for hostas that's been going on for the past fifty years. It still has great merit, but it also has many rivals, including 'Aurora Borealis', 'Great Expectations', 'Gold Standard', and 'Patriot'.

Flowers and foliage are by no means the only sources of color in a garden that is thoughtfully made, for certain plants please us throughout the year with their colorful stems or bark or with their fruit in autumn, which sometimes persists into winter.

Scotch broom, winter jasmine, and kerria sport emerald stems after leaf fall. There is great beauty in the exfoliating russet bark of *Lagerstroemia fauriei* and *Metasequoia glyptostroboides* and in the flaking gray-green bark of *Pinus bungeana,* which peels off to reveal the creamy yellow inner bark below. Red twig dogwood (*Cornus alba* 'Sibirica') is a sprawling, suckering shrub of moderate height that needs severe pruning every spring to keep it in bounds, but its crimson stems cheer the heart from late November to mid-March, especially when there is snow on the ground.

Then, in the ripening season of autumn, gardens may be beautiful with fruits and seeds: with the red berries of nandina and holly; with beautyberries and snowberries; with swelling quinces and apples and pears; with pomegranates and their seeds encased in translucent, brilliant ruby. The mahogany seed heads of tall sedums and echinops can be left standing all winter. They are espe-

Some perennials need not be cut back as winter arrives, for they can be lovely when snow falls on them, as here with echinops, or globe thistles.

One of the most carefree of all roses, Rosa rugosa *becomes especially lovely in the fall, when its great round hips turn bright scarlet.*

Another East Asian rose species, Rosa moyesii, *bears enormous crimson hips that are among the most spectacular fruits of autumn.*

cially lovely when snow falls on a calm day, topping them with little igloos of white.

Rose hips, particularly those of two Asian species, are by far the most spectacular fruits of the late year. The first—both in historical appearance and in overall garden appropriateness—is the wrinkled rose, *Rosa rugosa,* so named for the pleated or rugose texture of its dark green, glossy, disease-resistant foliage. Low and horrendously spiny, *Rosa rugosa* blooms over a long period with single flowers ranging from white through pink to purple. Probably native to north central Asia, it came to Japan from China some time around the tenth century. It is extremely hardy and tolerant of both drought and salt air. These qualities that have made it a rampant colonizer in northern coastal areas of Japan—and on Martha's Vineyard, where paths through the dunes leading to the beach are flanked with wooden snow fences and spreading masses of roses.

Rosa rugosa reached England early in the nineteenth century, America by 1872. *Rosa moyesii,* somewhat later in arriving, was collected in western China in 1890 and named with species status in 1906. Its single flowers are deep red, and its stems are comparatively spineless. The fruits of *Rosa moyesii* outshine those of *Rosa rugosa* by a good country mile. They are a glossy, smoldering crimson and up to two and a half inches from stem to tip. Anyone with room enough to grow this wild Chinese rose should do so, but room enough means lots and lots of it. I first saw this plant at Sissinghurst Castle in October about fifteen years ago. Seeing the hips, I whispered, "Wonderful!" But considering that they were borne on bushes fourteen feet high and almost as wide, I added, "But not for me." This rose was, in fact, almost too big for Sissinghurst.

The hips of these two wild roses bring us to another point in the progress of the gardener's eye, for they are distinct from one another and they cannot be mistaken for the fruits of any other plant. It is not their color alone that gives them their unmistakable beauty, but their form or shape. The slightly flattened hips of *Rosa rugosa* are fat and globular, and they are attended by the remnants of their calyxes, which flare out widely to give each fruit a form somewhat reminiscent of an octopus. Those of *Rosa moyesii* are long, attenuated, and shaped like jugs or flagons. When we proclaim these fruits to be beautiful, it is not just color that we are talking about, but their parts and the arrangement of these parts in combination with one another. Thus, from color, whether in flowers, foliage, or bark, we go on to develop an appreciative and educated eye for form and shape. It is form that identifies any plant as such, that makes it recognizable as what it is. To enjoy and appreciate color, the eye (or camera lens) need not be focused, and there is no necessity to name the objects that reflect the light. To appreciate form properly, vision must be sharpened and brought to bear on particular objects that have names to be learned.

Some flowers stand out so prominently for the way they are constructed that to see them once is always to know them. There is no room here to provide a full account of the beauty of form as it is exemplified in flowers, but a few examples may suffice to make the point.

Take passionflowers, for instance. They are so intricately wrought that Spanish missionaries to the New World saw in them a testament to Christ's crucifixion, with the five petals and five sepals standing for the ten apostles present at the event (Peter and Judas being otherwise occupied), the fringed corona the crown of thorns, the three styles the nails, and the tendrils the scourges used as whips. But no theological overlay is needed to see that these flowers are remarkable in every way.

The flowers of sea holly (Eryngium alpinum), *surrounded by a multitude of spiny bracts, are among the strangest in the plant kingdom, with the look of feather dusters or perhaps colonies of coral animals on ocean reefs.*

*P*assiflora coccinea, *the tropical red granadilla, shows the floral structures that early Spanish missionaries saw as emblematic of the crucifixion of Christ. Although the flowers last but a day, they have surpassing beauty of form. The edible fruit of the plant is used in drinks popular among tourists to the Caribbean.*

One glimpse of the white bracts of *Davidia involucrata,* so much like great birds that the origin of the common name dove tree is clear, is sufficient to know why the English nursery firm James Veitch and Sons dispatched E. H. Wilson to western China in 1900 with the main purpose of collecting its seeds.

The flame and canary color of the flowers of the climbing African lily, *Gloriosa superba* 'Rothschildiana', may be the initial attraction, but the eye then goes on to admire the stamens that flare out in a wide circle and the twisted, swept-back petals that together give these flowers the look of silken hot-air balloons about to ascend toward the heavens on a bright and sunny summer day.

The closely related genera *Datura* and *Brugmansia* contain a number of species with transcendent beauty of form. *Datura innoxia,* whose common names include angels' trumpets and moon lilies, is a shrub-like annual with velvety, grayish-green foliage of a pronouncedly musty scent. It blooms from late summer until early autumn, producing more and more large, erect buds every day. Standing like candles, they open toward dusk into lovely, upward-facing

The enormous, pendant flowers of the subtropical tree form of angels' trumpets (Brugmansia arborea) possess an elegance of form that is virtually matchless, but their beauty is coupled with danger, for they are extremely poisonous in every part.

The crown imperial (Fritillaria imperialis), which was brought to Europe from Asia Minor in early modern times, delights the eye with its pineapple topknot and its pendant bell-shaped flowers, each containing a large, gravity-defying drop of sweet nectar.

Fritillaria meleagris, the guinea-hen flower native to England and western Europe, has a sober charm all its own. Its tessellated bells are nowhere near as flamboyant as those of its crown-imperial cousin, but it has its enthusiastic partisans.

white flowers, much resembling those of moonflower vines, with a slightly bluish cast. Brugmansias, tropical plants that are called *la reina de la noche* ("queen of the night") in Latin America, are small trees that can produce many downward-facing trumpet-shaped blossoms at a time. (Of course neither daturas or brugmansias are suitable plants for gardens where small children are likely to play, for they are extremely poisonous in every part.)

The crown imperial, *Fritillaria imperialis,* is easily the most magnificently bold spring-flowering bulb. Rising eighteen inches or more above a low flurry of basal leaves, it opens its ring of brick-red (or sometimes yellow), large bell-like flowers below a topknot pineapple of twisted, swirling foliage.

There are too many highly distinctive flowers to describe them all, but a partial list would certainly include most magnolias, a great many orchids, night-blooming cereus and all epiphyllums, anthuriums, bearded iris, *Hibiscus rosa-sinensis* and many other plants in the Mallow family, and *Dicentra spectabilis,* the bleeding heart. I speak here, incidentally, only of those flowers that flaunt themselves like courtesans to the naked eye, or that represent a kind of garden pornography. A closer look at seemingly more modest blossoms with a hand lens opens up a further world of extraordinary floral form and shape: chickweed flowers are opulent beauties, and dandelion flowers look like they evolved in a distant galaxy.

Beauty of form is found in parts of flowers as well—in the velvety cloth of gold that forms the beard on the falls of an iris, in the starry pistil of a night-blooming cereus, in the incipient seed case at the heart of a lotus. The educated eye looks ever more deeply. It has not abandoned its old love affair with color, but appreciation of floral forms has enhanced it.

Leaves are almost endlessly variable in size and shape. In size they range from the tiny, feathery cladophylls of asparagus to the big, bold extravagances of the castor bean, the giant taro (*Alocasia macrorrhiza*), and, especially, *Gunnera manicata* (whose leaves make serviceable umbrellas). Leaves are multiform, and botanists know more words to describe their shapes than gardeners probably care to learn. They may be shaped like hands, hearts, or kidneys; like

*P*ollinated by beetles and one of the most ancient and primitive genera of all flowering plants, magnolias bear flowers that combine powerful fragrance with extremely arresting forms, as here with Magnolia sargentiana.

Seen from the side, as they ordinarily appear in bulb catalogs, tulips seem to be simple in form, one of many cup-shaped flowers. But to look closely into the very heart of a tulip is to discover a surprising complexity of form and anatomy. In this tulip—'Gudoshnik'— the eye is also treated to extremely subtle gradations of color.

blades, lances, needles, shields, spatulas, or spears. They may lack any quality of distinction ("just plain leaves") or they may be unique and instantly identifiable. They may be arranged opposite one another on their stems, may alternate with one another, or may be arranged like the steps of a spiral staircase. They may be made up of a few leaflets or a great many. They may, like the leaves of the traveler's palm, be arranged in a huge semicircle in a single vertical plane so that from a great distance they look like windmills. They may be as intricately pleated as an antique folding fan. Their veins may run parallel to one another from the base of the leaf or may radiate from a central vein, to describe just two of many possibilities. Their margins may be smooth, toothed like saws, or spiny with protective prickles or thorns.

Leaves may take part in the act of propagation. Some kalanchoes bear tiny embryonic plants in their leaf notches, and the leaves of the piggyback plant (*Tolmiea menziesii*) of the Pacific Northwest form new plants close to the point of connection with their stems. Leaves may even evolve, where soils are extremely weak in such nutrients as nitrogen, to trap prey. They derive energy

Poppies, like Papaver rhoeas, *combine brilliant color, exuberant and flouncing form, and an architectural complexity of stamens and seedpods, making them indispensable in early summer gardens, despite the brevity of their bloom.*

*The birdlike form of the individual segments of the columbine earns them not only that common name (for doves) but also birds-round-a-dish. This species is the native eastern columbine (*Aquilegia canadensis*)*

not just from the sun through photosynthesis, but also by luring, capturing, and digesting insects. (Some species of pitcher plant in the tropical genus *Nepenthes* can consume frogs and lizards, even mice and fair-sized rats.)

The contorted branches and twigs of the twisted hazel, *Corylus avellana* 'Contorta', spiral around one another and into thin air like someone searching for something rare and lost. During late spring and summer this shrub is covered with coarse and unattractive foliage, but in the winter, when the architecture of its stems and branches is revealed, it is a joy to see. Its waxy catkins help measure the progress of winter toward spring. Tiny at first, they steadily grow longer, until by mid-March they reach five or six inches. They sway and dangle in the slightest breeze, and when they finally release their ripe pollen, the air all around seems to shimmer with gold dust.

Of equal winter interest, and a favorite with flower arrangers, is the fantail pussy willow. It is, frankly, boring in summer, but when the leaves depart they reveal curving, oddly flattened or fasciated stems, which look as if they've been hammered. The bark is a richly burnished dark mahogany red. When the catkins begin swelling in late winter, they are so soft and satisfying to touch or stroke that pussy willow seems almost an inevitable common name.

In this chapter thus far, I have singled out a goodly number of plants, which I grow on a small suburban lot. But the main point is not that I grow them: it is that I grow them *in a garden.* The attention of gardeners often focuses on plants in their singularity—on the stunning indigo blue flowers of *Salvia guaranitica* or the glowing garnet ones of *S. vanhouttii;* on the glossy, waxen leaves of *Asarum europaeum* or the pale green, pleated foliage of *Alchemilla mollis,* on which dewdrops gleam like diamonds in early morning; on the cranberry-tipped blades of the lovely grass *Imperata cylindrica* 'Rubra' when they are back-lit in the golden light of late afternoon. But a garden is more than a collection of plants of singular and individual merit. All gardens, great and small, aspire toward fine art. They differ in how well they achieve their goal, but the goal is the same: an ensemble of plants that is visually satisfying. Such an ensemble has one precondition: it can come only from an eye that is thoroughly educated and long practiced.

The first essential for putting together such an ensemble is extremely simple: the plants must grow well. Another essential is knowing what plants can be expected to grow and thrive in a particular garden, with its particular conditions. But there is no art in choosing plants on the sole criterion of their ability to thrive on a given piece of real estate. The art of gardening is the art of combining plants aesthetically. The choices that must be made are extremely complex. They are also personal, admitting of few real rules and many exceptions.

When, for example, is the garden to be at its peak of bloom? Some gardeners aim for a single season. It may be spring, with its brief explosion of color from bulbs, woodland ephemerals like mertensias and tiarellas and trilliums, and flowering shrubs and trees. It may be summer, for its long display of a succession of perennials in herbaceous borders—and its almost unending generosity of bloom from annuals. It may be autumn, so rich in perennial asters, eupatoriums, salvias, sedums, sunflowers (and, of course, chrysanthemums). Some gardeners, it must be said, wish to avoid having a peak of bloom. They prefer a slow unfolding through all four seasons—including winter, with its winter-flowering heaths, its snowdrops, and its hellebores. To achieve a four-season garden, they forgo a bright spectacle in every corner at any one time.

Another question that all gardeners must answer for themselves concerns the balance between the garden as an integrated whole and the garden as a home for collections of plants that are the objects of a private passion. Some of us fall in love with particular sorts of plants, as I have already pointed out. The objects of our affection can be almost anything—rhododendrons, roses, sempervivums, you name it. We collect as many species and cultivars of our favorites as we can. These must find a home in our gardens, but accommodating sixty different hosta cultivars or twenty of David Austin's new English shrub roses means, inevitably, a loss of diversity in the garden as a whole. On the other hand, opting for diversity means giving up the luxury of indulging particular passions, even whims. You make your choices and you pay the price, whatever the choices may be.

In any art there are degrees of talent, there is long practice in getting things right, and there are degrees of achievement. So it is with the art of gardening. Some people have a more perceptive eye than others. Some labor long to take every advantage of their natural gift. They may make many mistakes along the way, but they know that a mistake is not a tragedy. This year's mistakes, if recognized, are lessons that teach next year's improvements.

The principles of putting it all together, of combining *plants* to make a *garden*, are so well known—or at least so often expressed in books on design—as to be almost commonplace. We have heard them all dozens and dozens of times in gardening talks and symposia. And yet a garden where all these principles (there aren't many) are entirely embodied is so rare as to be almost instantly recognizable and to provoke immediate admiration: this gardener knows what he or she is doing!

Here, in summary, are just a few of the principles:

The goal is diversity, but diversity within an overall unity. Diversity is not restricted to having a great many genera and their species and cultivars, although that's part of the matter. Diversity also means attending to the growth habits of plants, playing them off against one another on the one hand, and allowing them to echo one another on the other. Some plants are gumdrops (grow in mounds), others are steeples (grow vertically). Most gardens are dominated by gumdrops (and probably should be), but all gardens need their steeples and spires, or their exclamation points.

Diversity also means giving due consideration to the effects of foliage. Leaves come to us in a great variety of sizes, shapes, and textures which may be played off against one another very effectively, in two opposing ways.

One is contrast, and the other is repetition.

Contrast is important because the royal road to dullness, in gardening as in anything else, is monotony. In his delightful *Elements of Garden Design* (1996), Joe Eck tells the instructive tale of a British gardener, vaguely dissatisfied with her meticulously tended garden, who called in a noted plantsman to diagnose what might be wrong. After carefully observing the garden, he struck to the heart of the problem, telling her, "Your leaves are all the same size." Such uniformity of leaf size can easily happen, given the fact that the leaves of many plants tend to be of an unremarkable size, neither especially tiny nor especially large. There is a great deal of room for playing Mutt and Jeff with foliage, once the principle of diversity is acknowledged. Something delicate and tiny can be placed near something bold and dramatic—say, *Lonicera nitida* with its finely wrought tiny leaves adjacent to a castor bean or, perhaps, if the soil be moist and the winter climate gentle, a massive stand of *Gunnera manicata* with its enormous leaves. In a garden where vegetables are used as ornamentals, a fine, dramatic clump of one of the handsomer selections of rhubarb, maybe *Rheum palmatum* 'Atrosanguineum', could be faced down with double rows of grassy and narrow-leafed chives at its feet.

In Susan Ryley's highly imaginative and well-designed garden in Victoria, British Columbia, plantings are put together with the deliberate intent to make them have a pictorial quality from inside the house.

One window looking onto the terrace of the Ryley garden features a planting that demonstrates enormously sophisticated taste in plant combination. Buddleia 'Harlequin' consorts with Euphorbia sikkimensis *and* Lobelia tupa.

*T*he pool on Ryley's terrace features water lilies and angels' fishing rods (Dierama pulcherrima).

The same principle applies to texture. Ferny or feathery foliage can be combined with less complicated leaves, to the huge advantage of each. Two such combinations that I have shamelessly plagiarized from friends' gardens are bronze fennel with cardoons and red chard with asparagus. I also immensely admire a planting Marco Polo Stufano contrived some years ago at Wave Hill, where he combined feathery and graceful asparagus, pennisetums, and miscanthus with the much bolder forms of giant elephant ears and tall cannas. (This combination was not only elegant and lovely, but something of a botanical pun: all these plants are monocots.)

Need I even mention diversity of flower forms? A garden composed of nothing but daisies would be monumentally tedious. (It would also be extremely easy to come by, considering the popularity and availability of asters, boltonias, chrysanthemums, purple coneflowers, coreopsis, dahlias, erigerons, heleniums, helianthuses, gloriosa daisies and other rudbeckias, and dozens of additional composites.)

But the element of contrast must be balanced by that of repetition. Without

The Ryley garden sports a terrific combination of crinodonnas and variegated phlox 'Norah Leigh'.

repetition, contrasting leaf sizes, shapes, and textures become jittery and frenetic, allowing the eye no place to rest and reassure itself. The same plant may be repeated in the garden plan—or plants that are similar to one another may be added to provide echoes or variations on a theme. (Thus the fine-textured leaves of sweet woodruff might be paired with the similarly shaped but larger leaves of marsh marigold.)

The symmetry of formal gardens fairly assures the presence of a large degree of repetition. For such gardens, particular attention needs to be paid to contrast. Conversely, informal gardens are likely to be abundant with contrast. For these, garden makers should carefully plan for repetition. In both, the important thing is balance.

Another goal is the integration of the garden with the house it surrounds. In this matter, Americans have huge liabilities to overcome. Since the Civil War, and especially since the rapid suburbanization that occurred after World War II, the dominant pattern of residential architecture has placed the house square in the middle of its lot, with a yard out back and another yard out front, clearly intended for a lawn open to the street. In the 1950s, many social critics commented on the peculiarity of bay or picture windows set into the fronts of houses, looking out toward . . . the similar windows of the house across the street. (I have always been a little confused by the ambiguity of the "picture" in the "picture window." Is it the scene that the inhabitants of a house see when

*S*usan Ryley's terrace garden features a sophisticated combination of a great diversity of plant textures, colors, and forms.

they are inside looking out? Or is it the scene the passerby sees from the sidewalk or the street?)

Whatever the case, solid walls dominate in most such domestic architecture, for one good reason: they provide the privacy that is a casualty of having a front lawn open to the street. Something extremely interesting happens once a decision is made to enclose an ordinary suburban lot, perhaps by planting a thicket of mixed tall grasses, shrubs, and small trees around its periphery (as I did many years ago). In time, the urge is irresistible to open the house to the garden, the garden to the house—to build decks or patios next to the house; to replace the visual barriers of walls with the transparency of glass, with more generous windows and French doors. The results are astounding, as house and garden flow together into a single private and intimate space. The garden becomes a yearlong companion to the house, not just a spring and summer procession going on outside. How the garden looks from various vantage points inside the house comes to be a major consideration in choosing and siting plants.

Correct—even inspired—casting (to borrow a metaphor from films, opera, and theater) *is a third objective.* Choosing the plants for an ensemble is like selecting the players for a performance of a grand opera. Most are members of the orchestra and chorus or extras carrying spears. All, nevertheless, are essential and must be carefully cast. The divas and heroic tenors ought to be extraordinarily fine, for when they are onstage, every eye is on them, every ear listening. The divas of a garden are generally woody plants of such distinction that they strike the eye with an immediate force. One returns to them again and again, contemplating them with entire satisfaction.

Among opera lovers, particular stars have their fervent admirers, who may argue among themselves. The three outstanding tenors of today are all great, but which one is the greatest? The choice is ultimately personal, as is the choice of those plants that will play a starring role in a garden. I have some favorites. Among those I do not grow are *Pyrus salicifolia* 'Pendula' (the stunning but difficult to find weeping silver pear) and the weeping katsura tree, *Cercidiphyllum magnificum* 'Pendulum', which looks like a cascade of blue-green in summer, and of flame in autumn, yet has none of the weeping willow's atrocious habits of invading and clogging water lines and dropping brittle branches in all seasons. *Aralia elata* 'Variegata' has entranced me ever since I first saw it growing in John and Billie Elsley's garden in South Carolina. A small shrubby tree, it has massive compound leaves edged in cream with overtones and brushings of pink, and it produces frothy panicles of creamy white flowers in late summer. It is winter- and summer-hardy over a wide range, from New England through the lower South.

The two favorites I do grow are a red threadleaf Japanese maple of unknown identity and a weeping mulberry, *Morus alba* 'Pendula'. It took Hella and me fifteen years to find the latter, although mature weeping mulberries abound in neighborhood gardens going back to late Victorian times. In all seasons, this small tree is a gorgeous, sculptural sight. In summer, its flowing branches are covered with large glossy leaves. In winter, bare and deep gray, it looks like a frozen waterfall.

Every garden is unique, and every garden embodies and witnesses to the creative vision of its maker. It cannot be otherwise. Written English makes use of an alphabet of only twenty-six letters, spoken English a larger, but still comparatively limited set of phonemes, or individual sounds. Out of such meager materials we have built all of our poetry, all of our philosophy, all of our law, all of our communications with one another, save those which we express by gesture, body language, and the movements of our facial muscles. The elements of the language of gardening, in comparison with those of written and spoken language, are vast, and their permutations, in the choices we make of what to plant and where, are infinite. The material of our art and craft is life itself in all its variety.

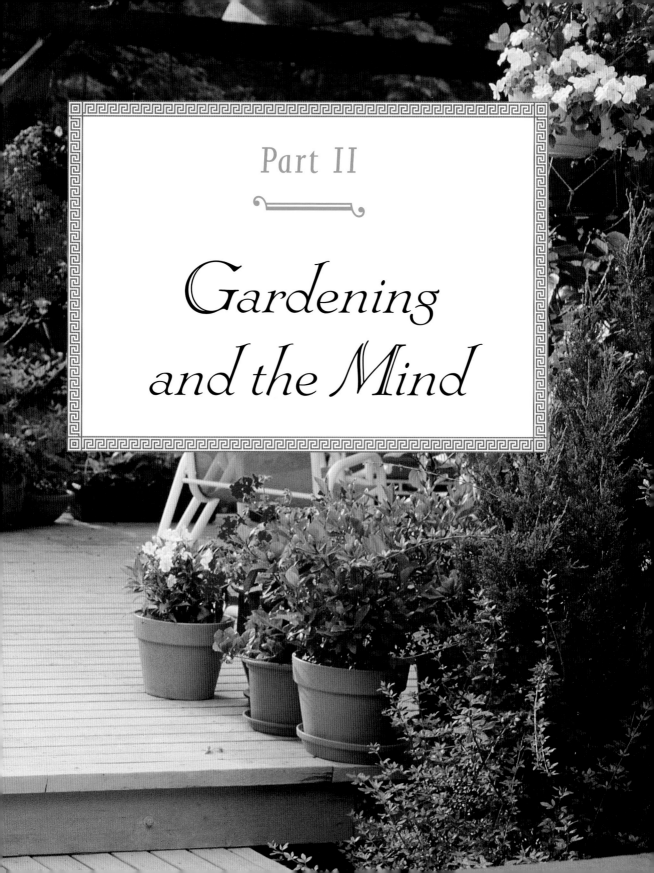

Part II

Gardening and the Mind

Introduction

In addition to all its rich offerings to the body and its five senses, gardening engages the mind. It offers the intellect more than it can even partially fathom during a long lifetime.

In a certain way, this point has been suggested already in the preceding pages. Talking about seeing or hearing or any other kind of perception is not itself a sensory experience, but a mental activity. When we see a gardenia and bend over to inhale its rich perfume, we do so because we *already know* it will have such a perfume. Either we discovered it on our own at some time in the past, or someone taught us. ("Here, smell this flower.") Furthermore, in these pages so far there's been what might be called, not very precisely, a lot of stuff. Thomas Jefferson made an appearance. So did Queen Anne, Helen Keller, and a good many other people. (The philosophers René Descartes and David Hume were in an early draft, until someone suggested that a book about gardening probably wasn't the right venue for observations about the differences between French rationalism and English empiricism.) A considerable number of plants were named, sometimes with both common and scientific names, and knowing what something is called qualifies unmistakably as knowledge. Finally, I left untouched several areas of inquiry pertaining to the senses as regards gardens and much else besides. In regard to the sense of smell, for example, I didn't take up the several systems of classifying particular kinds of smell, starting with Linnaeus's proposal of seven groups (aromatic, fragrant, ambrosial, alliaceous,

hircine, foul, and nauseating) and concluding with much more recent propos-
als from chemists of a different seven (camphoraceous, musky, floral, peppermint, ethereal, pungent, and putrid). I didn't discuss the physics of smell (which
has to do with the shapes of volatile molecules) or its physiology in humans (a
matter of olfactory receptors in our nasal passages). If I were writing a book
dealing solely with fragrance and gardens, there might have been room to take
up these and many other topics of inquiry and areas of knowledge.

The transaction between gardening and the mind is a vast, virtually infinite
subject, but books are finite. I will accordingly limit myself in the pages that follow in this part of the book to some of the things that can be known about our
patch of earth on the coastal plain of southern New Jersey.

I write in a second-floor study that overlooks part of the back garden,
although my view of most of it is blocked by a quince tree, whose branches on
this midsummer day are beginning to bend under the weight of its golden,
downy fruit. I am not exactly alone in this study, for there are nine bookcases,
all but one floor-to-ceiling. Roughly half the books on the shelves deal with
plants and gardens. I just counted them. Totaling 693, they contain more sheer
information than anyone could ever assimilate, as well as a wealth of opinion
and sometimes prejudice. Reference books, books on garden history East and
West, facsimiles of English herbals from the seventeenth century, memoirs of
plant collectors and explorers, collections of essays, scholarly monographs on
particular plant genera—a great deal of material on the world of plants and
gardens is to be found in this good-sized horticultural library built up book by
book over a period of more than thirty years.

In the earlier pages of this book, I argued that a garden worthy of the name
is a retreat from the world. Now I mean to show a few of the many ways in
which in one small garden on a midsummer day, the entire world is to be found.

CHAPTER 6

To Speak of Quinces

Any garden, even a small one like ours, offers more than enough to occupy the mind, in an intellectual quest with no stopping point. To understand everything that goes on in our garden would be to understand virtually the entire universe. I would have to be intimately acquainted with botany and geology and entomology, and with the complex interrelationships between plants and their environment and its other inhabitants. I would need to know about DNA; about atmospheric gases; about photosynthesis; about nastic movements and thigmotropism—and all of these just for starters. I would have to learn French and Russian and Chinese and Japanese, at a minimum. I would have to brush up on Latin and Greek and considerably improve my scientific German. I would have to haunt libraries for years, subscribe to hundreds of learned journals, attend dozens of symposia and conferences each year. Recent technology would require much frequenting of the Internet—and of whatever may come along to supplant it. Even then, I would still understand only a tiny fraction of what plants and gardens invite the mind and intellect to explore. The topics that arise in the effort to understand what goes on in a garden are, quite simply, inexhaustible.

But let me illustrate this point by focusing attention on just one plant in my garden—any plant will do, so I'll just pick arbitrarily that quince tree outside my window—and considering what might be known about it. Since every piece of knowledge can be understood as an answer to a question, I will ask: what questions might we ask about this quince?

The first question, of course, is, What's it called? Two kinds of answer might be given. One is a common name—in this case, "quince." The other kind of answer is a Latin binomial, with the first word capitalized but not the second, and with both words either underlined or printed in italics. In this particular case, *Cydonia oblonga*—or, more precisely, *Cydonia oblonga* Mill.

At first glance, at least in the case of my quince, its common name and its Latin name seem to be on a par, equally precise, meaningful, and unambiguous. If anything, its common name has the advantage of being simple and straightforward. It may be difficult to imagine John Wayne saying that his quince was in bloom, but it's transcendently impossible to imagine him saying anything about his *Cydonia oblonga*. It sounds show-offy, sissy, and downright un-

While still on the tree, quinces are covered with a protective golden down that washes off at harvest, to reveal their waxen, deep green skin. As they continue to ripen, they turn a rich apricot hue. [PHOTO BY ALLEN LACY]

American. But there are problems nevertheless with "quince," thanks to the "flowering quince." The quince outside my window flowers every spring—and very nicely too, with large, pale pink single blossoms that are handsome against its fresh new gray-green foliage—but it is not a "flowering quince." I have one of those in the front garden, and it's a different plant altogether. My quince is a Eurasian plant that has long been in cultivation in the West. My flowering quince hails from Japan, and it wasn't grown in Europe or America until after 1800. Any confusion between the two plants vanishes if we call one *Cydonia oblonga* and the other *Chaenomeles japonica*. (But there is still confusion about the common name of the *Chaenomeles*. Gardeners down south—also in England—don't call it "flowering quince." Instead, it's "japonica bush" or simply "japonica." We know what we mean when we talk about our japonicas, but when we do so we can read bewilderment on the faces of people from other parts of the country.)

Turning for the moment from quinces and japonicas to other plants and their common names, we find even greater nomenclatural chaos. *The same plant can have several, even many, different common names.* Take daffodils, for instance. They are called "Lent lilies" in some parts of England (although they aren't lilies), and in Tennessee some people call them "buttercups." Elsewhere in the south, all daffodils are often referred to as "jonquils," although that name properly refers only to one particular kind of daffodil, one whose flowers in late spring have an uncommonly sweet perfume. *Different plants can share the same common name.* If you grow up in a part of Tennessee where daffodils are "buttercups" and venture into other parts of the English-speaking world, you'll soon discover that almost anything with yellow flowers will be a buttercup to someone or other. There's another difficulty with common names. Although many a plant has several of them, *some don't have any at all.* For centuries now, our gardens have been almost unimaginably enriched by plants newly discovered and collected in the remotest corners of the earth. Never known and never grown before, they arrive unchristened in our hands, bereft of any folk names by which to call them.

Confusion is compounded when gardeners speak different languages. Hardy cyclamens are "sow's bread" in English, "Alpenveilchen" (alpine violets) in German. A literal translation from one language to another would be a mistranslation. Even when the literal meaning is the same, the words used to express this meaning are different. A common name in English for impatiens is "busy Lizzie," which in German coincides almost exactly with "fleissige Lieschen," but the match would not be evident to anyone who did not know both languages as well as the plant referred to. And, getting back to my quince, to a German it's not a quince at all but a *Quitte*. An American and a German gardener cannot communicate with each other about their quince trees unless one of them has bothered to learn the other's native tongue.

There is another alternative, of course. Both gardeners could learn to use a third language, a lingua franca. In early modern times, the most obvious candidate for such a language was Latin, and indeed Latin became the universal language of the rapidly developing science of botany—the organized body of systematic knowledge of plants. Latin, however, was often cumbersome, as in this seventeenth-century attempt to name the garden carnation with a descriptive tag: "*Dianthus floribus solitariis, squamis calycinis subovatis brevissimus, corollis crenatis.*"

The garden carnation today, fortunately, is denoted by just two words in Latin: *Dianthus caryophyllus* L. We have left the realm of common names altogether and entered the orderly world of Latin binomials. Common names, as we have seen, have all the linguistic untidiness that is symbolized by the biblical story of the building of the Tower of Babel—an adventure in civic architecture whose outcome was the loss of the universal language on which human cooperation and mutual understanding depended. The Latin binomial is a different beast altogether than the common name, with none of its inherent difficulties. It is the same in any language. Whether you say of *Iris pallida* that it's "beautiful," "schön," or "bonita," it's *Iris pallida* that you're talking about. Binomial names are unambiguous. Their custodians—we call them botanical taxonomists—have taken pains to make certain that this is so. Botanical names are precise and exact. Such names, furthermore, show relationships between particular kinds of plants, without suggesting relationships that don't exist. No matter what word comes after *Quercus,* it's some kind of oak that we're talking about (and poison oak doesn't belong in the conversation: it's a *Toxicodendron*). And if common names are parceled out so unevenly that the greater number of plants don't have even one, much less several, botanical names are rationed out with a fine evenhandedness. Every plant, in theory at least, has its precise and correct scientific name, even if today countless species of plants in the tropical rain forests of the world are marching into extinction before they have been named and scientifically studied, in a disaster of enormous proportions.

I feel a huge temptation here to digress, to consider the plight of the tropical rain forests, its causes, and its probable consequences; to sing an anthem for the cause of biodiversity; to teach what I can of what I know about this matter. I will resist the temptation, but point out that it exists and point out further that in a few short paragraphs, we have moved from a question concerning the name of just one plant in my garden to an environmental question of global significance. This is always the way with a garden: it opens into a much larger world.

But another question now intrudes itself. How did we get those botanical names for plants? I will skip entirely the early history of plant naming, cutting directly to Carolus Linnaeus (1707–1778), the Swedish botanist who gave every living thing he could get his hands on a binomial Latin name (including himself: he was born Carl von Linné). Linnaeus did not invent the practice of using Latin names. After all, the ancient Romans did so every time they opened their mouths. Furthermore, almost everyone who wrote about plants and gardens before Linnaeus came along used Latin names for plants, even if what they had to say about them was in English, French, German, or some other language. Sometimes such names were binomial, but often they went on at considerable and cumbersome length, as we have already seen with the garden carnation.

Linnaeus cleared up all the confusion surrounding plant names by developing a system of binomial nomenclature whereby organisms are identified by their genus and their species. In this system, one kind of plant would have its own name, and only one name, and this name would not be used for any other kind of plant. All names would consist of two words in Latin, followed by an initial or proper name identifying the person who first gave a particular plant its name. In a truly amazing burst of nomenclatural energy, Linnaeus named in just twelve months 5,900 genera and species, before publishing his *Species Plantarum* in 1753.

There are two important questions about Linnaeus's system. First, how did he classify plants, assigning each its genus and species? Second, where did he get the names he assigned?

His basic system of classification was based on counting the sexual organs of flowers—the numbers of stamens (or styles) and pistils they displayed, from one stamen and one pistil to many of each. Further refinements resulted in a complex, but rational and understandable, ordering of the world of plants. In a sense, Linnaeus was a second Adam, taking on himself the first task God assigned Adam. (Genesis 2: 16, 19: "And the Lord God took the man, and put him in the garden of Eden to dress it and keep it; . . . then brought unto him every living creature to see what he would call it, and whatsoever Adam called every living creature, that was the name thereof.")

In botanical reference books, the names Linnaeus gave are indicated by the initial L. His names came from a variety of sources. Some were the old Latin common names for particular kinds of plants—*Acer* for maples, *Quercus* for oaks, *Salix* for willows. Some binomial names were shortened forms of traditional Latin descriptive names running to three or more words. Some plants not native to Europe, which of course would not have had traditional common names in Latin, received made-up names. For the North American sweet gum tree, Linnaeus invented the hauntingly mellifluous *Liquidambar styraciflua,* from the Latin words for liquid and amber, and for flowing styrax, the aromatic resin the tree produces.

Some names came from people—botanists in particular, especially Swedish botanists. North American mountain laurel was named *Kalmia* for Pehr Kalm, one of Linnaeus's students. *Rudbeckia* was named for one of Linnaeus's teachers, Olaus Rudbeck (1630–1702), who had been professor of botany at the University of Uppsala. Linnaeus named one genus, *Moraea,* a South African member of the Iris family, in honor of Sara Lisa Moraeus, whom he later married. Linnaeus even named one plant, *Linnaea borealis,* for himself, describing it as "a plant of Lapland, lowly, insignificant, disregarded, flowering but for a brief space—from Linnaeus who resembles it."

Later botanists continued the patterns of naming that Linnaeus established, including naming plants for people. Some names honor figures in public life, who may or may not have had botanical leanings. Some of the early political leaders of the United States gave their names to plants, with the genera *Franklinia, Jeffersonia,* and *Washingtonia. Lewisia* and *Clarkia* take their names from Lewis and Clark, the leaders of an expedition to the Pacific Northwest whose purpose in part was to bring east specimens of that region's flora. One

such plant was the *Mahonia,* named for the nurseryman Bernard M'Mahon.

Plant names also open up a larger world of ancient history and mythology. *Eupatorium,* a genus that includes the American wildflower Joe Pye weed, was named for Mithridates Eupator, king of Pontus. *Liriope* takes its name from a Greek nymph of woodlands. *Euryale,* a water lily native to India, was named for one of the Gorgons, who like her sister Medusa had poisonous snakes for hair. The lovely poet's or Alexandrian laurel, *Danaë racemosa,* takes its genus name from Danaë, who was ravished by Zeus appearing as a shower of gold, thus siring Perseus.

We have only begun to explore the questions that follow our original query about the name of my quince, for we could proceed much further into the world of nomenclature according to Linnaeus and his successors. We could move downward into subclassifications within his binomial systems, considering subspecies, forms, varieties, and other lesser divisions. Or we could move upward, considering plant families and other even larger units. We could, in other words, abandon gardening almost altogether, taking up botany instead. Or we could just take a tour around my garden, identifying every plant that grows there, including the weeds, with the proper botanical name (a task that would consume several hours at least). But I will turn instead to other questions about that quince, or any other plant in my garden.

For example, can it hurt me in some way? Some plants have the capacity to do us harm. Eat the wrong part of a plant with some edible parts, and the consequences can be grim. The seeds and leaves of avocados are poisonous. You may not die if you eat them, but you will be very sick. Eat a castor bean seed, and you have just ingested a potentially lethal dose of ricin, one of the most violently toxic chemicals on earth. Eat any part of an oleander, a monkshood, or a hellebore and you are flirting with the undertaker. Touch a leaf of bull nettle and you will think you have been stung by hornets. Brush up against poison ivy, and if you are susceptible to its toxic oil, urushiol, you are in for a bad time of it later. Handle the fruits of many plants in the *Capsicum,* or pepper, genus and then rub your eyes without first washing your hands and you will be very sorry very quickly. These are only a few examples of the harm that may come from being ignorant of some characteristics of certain plants.

Or, I may ask, can a plant help me in some way? In the case of my quince, the answer is yes. Its tart fruits are delicious once they ripen and are simmered for preserves or baked like apples with sugar and lemon juice. I have no doubt that they are nutritious as well: an ancient Roman proverb advised that "quinces not only yield pleasure, but also health." Quinces are but one of the earth's pleasant fruits, if hardly chief among them.

It would take many volumes even to begin to enumerate the blessings that plants bring us. The prophet Isaiah wrote, "All flesh is grass." He meant these words metaphorically, in reference to the transitoriness of human life, but the statement is literally true. Even inveterate carnivores who avoid eating anything that has sap flowing through it instead of blood must ultimately eat grass, because somewhere in the food chain below them some other creature is placidly grazing. The realization that all flesh is grass carries with it an even deeper truth: through photosynthesis, plants (and only plants) transform the sun's energy into other forms of energy that can be used by other kinds of life. Plants also absorb carbon dioxide and give off the oxygen that for 1,800 million years has been the life's breath of all living creatures (except for a few anaerobic organisms).

Although all life depends in one way or another on plants, human beings are plant dependent to the greatest degree and in the most diverse ways. Plants provide us with food, fiber for clothing and shelter, dye to color cloth, medicines for healing, and many other benefits. At least part of the fossil fuels that are still major sources of energy for industrial societies derive from the remains of plants that flourished many millions of years ago. Plants help control erosion from wind and water that would otherwise put all our precious topsoil at the bottom of the sea. An old bumper sticker reminded us, "Have you thanked a green plant today?" This sentiment still holds. The greatest imaginable catastrophe would be a virus that destroyed chlorophyll. It would swiftly turn Earth into a dead planet.

We may also ask of a plant, What is its history? Every plant has one, whether we know it or not. Take the regal lilies that bloom in my garden, for example. The story behind them is just one part of the personal history of an Englishman named Ernest H. Wilson.

Seen here on the steps of the main building of Harvard University's Arnold Arboretum, Ernest H. Wilson was one of the leading plant explorers and collectors of the twentieth century. [PHOTOGRAPHIC ARCHIVES OF THE ARNOLD ARBORETUM]

Wilson (1876–1930) looms large in twentieth-century American and British horticulture. He began collecting in China for the Arnold Arboretum in the early 1900s, after previously doing so for James Veitch and Sons, an English nursery company. Wilson's East Asian introductions include sixty rhododendron species, many ornamental flowering cherries, *Acer griseum, Davidia involucrata, Kolkwitzia amabilis, Lonicera nitida,* and *Sinarundinaria murielae,* a hardy clumping bamboo he named for his daughter Muriel. One of his greatest introductions was the regal lily (*Lilium regale*), whose discovery he described as follows in his memoir, *A Naturalist in Western China* (1913):

In the Min Valley the charming *Lilium regale* luxuriates in rocky crevices, sun-baked throughout the greater part of the year. It

Taken by E. H. Wilson, this photograph shows the rugged character of the remote areas in China where he collected such important garden plants as regal lilies. [PHOTOGRAPHIC ARCHIVES OF THE ARNOLD ARBORETUM]

grows 3 to 5 feet tall, and has slender leaves crowded on stems bearing several large funnel-shaped flowers, red-purple without, ivory-white suffused with canary-yellow within, often with the red-purple reflected through, and is deliciously fragrant.

Wilson's account of discovering this lily provides a vivid example of the hardships he and other plant explorers often had to endure in difficult terrain in searching out new plants for Western gardens:

There in narrow, semi-arid valleys down which torrents thunder, and encompassed by mountains composed of mudshales and granites, whose peaks are closed with snow eternal, the Regal Lily has its home. In summer the heat is terrific, in winter the cold is intense, and at all seasons these valleys are subject to

In the Oregon garden of Cynthia Woodyard, Ernest H. Wilson's regal lilies combine nicely with tall verbascums and giant alliums.

The dove tree (Davidia involucrata) is another of China's contributions to Western gardens that we owe to E. H. Wilson's several collecting expeditions.

sudden and violent windstorms against which neither man nor beast can make headway. There, in June, by the wayside, in rock-crevices by the torrent's edge, and high up on the mountainside, this lily in full bloom greets the weary wayfarer. Not in twos and threes but in hundreds, aye, in tens of thousands. . . . The air in the cool of the morning and in the evening is laden with delicious perfume exhaled from each bloom. For a brief season, this lonely semi-desert is transformed by this Lily into a veritable fairy-land.

This discovery took place in 1903. Wilson gave the Veitch nursery some bulbs, which flowered for the first time in England in 1905.

In September 1910, the regal lily almost cost Wilson his life. He had returned to China to collect bulbs of *Lilium regale* for the Arnold Arboretum, and he narrowly missed being swept away (and did break his leg badly) in a landslide on a treacherous trail above the Min River. Some 6,000 bulbs were dug that October, shipped 2,000 miles across China to Shanghai, and then sent via Vancouver, British Columbia, to Boston, where they arrived in April. They bloomed in July—the first regal lilies Americans had ever seen.

Other plants have a less dramatic history, but a history nonetheless. Consider, for example, the many daylilies that brighten my garden for many weeks in midsummer. The several species of *Hemerocallis* from which they descend are pleasant but fairly unexciting garden perennials, with narrow petals and a color range that can be summed up as yellow and muddy orange. But early in our century such pioneer hybridizers as Dr. Arlow B. Stout of the New York Botanical Garden began working to improve daylilies, suspecting that the genus had great potential. Daylilies are a hybridizer's dream, for they produce seed abundantly and bloom in their second year. They also increase rapidly by division, so that breeders can share particularly promising cultivars with one another. Dr. Stout named and introduced a number of his hybrids. A great many other hybridizers all over the United States followed in his footsteps. In time daylilies were transformed from rather plain Cinderellas of the summer garden into elegant prima donnas. Narrow petals gave way to wide, overlapping ones, often ruffled and flounced. Flowers with contrasting eye zones turned up. New flower forms appeared, closer to wide, flat disks than to the trumpet shapes typical of the original species Stout had worked with. But the most obvious transformation of daylilies was in the colors of their flowers. Pinks and melons emerged, and pale shades almost describable as white. The color purple turned up, also shades of wine, mauve, lavender, and lilac. Reds arrived, everything from reddish orange to dark, smoldering crimsons. The daylily patch came to resemble the iris patch, with the same rainbow colors of the spectrum, save for the blues that are common in iris but absent thus far in daylilies.

Beginning in the 1950s, some hybridizers began tinkering with the chromosome numbers of daylilies, treating germinating seedlings with the highly dangerous and carcinogenic chemical, colchicine, a derivative of the autumn-blooming bulb, *Colchicum.* Most of the seedlings died, but in some of the survivors, thanks to the momentary effect of colchicine in interrupting cell division, chromosome count had doubled. A new race of tetraploid daylilies emerged—and with it open warfare broke out between the breeders of the older, diploid plants and the advocates of tetraploids. The tet folks trumpeted that the day of the diploid had passed: twice the chromosomes meant an exponential increase in permutations. Furthermore, anyone could see that tetraploid flowers had better substance than diploid ones. Meanwhile, the diploid tribe disparaged the tets they had seen. Instead of the graceful, rather grassy foliage typical of daylilies, tetraploids had coarse, inelegant leaves. The greater substance of their flowers made them likely to cook in the afternoon sun, turning to mush. The battle between the two camps raged for some years, but now it has subsided. Some people still breed only diploids, some only tetraploids, and some both kinds. Both are offered in the catalogs of leading daylily nurseries. In the daylily world, there is peaceful coexistence—and the common recognition that both kinds have their particular merit.

I have summarized this history of daylilies in America, where most hybridization of the genus has been carried out, without mentioning anyone except A. B. Stout. The reason is simple. The names of the hybridizers who collectively have turned daylilies into virtually indispensable garden perennials are legion. Some were professional plantsmen, but most were keen amateurs from every walk of life. Butchers, telephone company executives, homemakers, physi-

The flowers of the opium poppy (Papaver somniferum) *may be single or double, and they range in color from white to pink to lavender and mauve. Traditionally the flowers of sleep and death, they bear seedpods with a latex sap that is the source of many drugs that are at once a blessing and a curse to human beings.*

cians, plumbers, lawyers, college professors of English, electricians—all have devoted their time, their energy, and above all their passion to the breeding of daylilies. The result is a truly bewildering number of named hybrids—over 35,000 at last count—from which gardeners may chose. None of these hybridizers, as far as I know, ever risked his or her life in a landslide like E. H. Wilson, but they all deserve our gratitude nonetheless.

In over twenty-five years I have learned much about the garden Hella and I have worked to bring into being. I do not claim to have complete knowledge—and in fact I wonder what such knowledge would be like. I would have to know by name every plant that grows here, including weeds and mosses. I would have to know how each plant fits within the systematic science that is botany—to know, for example, that my quince is a member of the Rose family, and thus kin not only to roses but also to apples, peaches, pears, and strawberries. I would have to know the history of all these plants—where on this globe they originally evolved, and by what chain of human transactions they arrived in our hands for our care.

Even if I were to succeed in the task of arriving at perfect knowledge of every plant on this small piece of earth, of the entire flora of my garden, my knowledge would still be fragmentary, because it would not embrace the fauna with which I share my garden. At present, on a midsummer day, there are many songbirds that we strive to attract and feed. A number of squirrels amuse us with their aerial acrobatics, and chipmunks frolic on our deck. Some mice have taken up residence inside my lawn mower, just above the blade. The insect population living here is by any reckoning unimaginably large. I am consciously aware of only a fraction of it—those insects that force themselves upon consciousness in ways that cannot be ignored: the annoying gnats, flies, mosquitoes, and yellow jackets that I could wish might permanently disappear; the aphids, mealy bugs, and spider mites that ravage choice plants to my displeasure and distress; the lovely butterflies that float like bright-colored little angelic beings above the flowers that attract their compound eyes as well as my simpler ones; the ants that I anthropomorphize into symbols of diligence and foresight, and the grasshoppers that I see as teaching the lesson that life has a winter to prepare for as well as a summer to enjoy; the honeybees and bumblebees that buzz by day through the flower beds and the lightning bugs that flash their phosphorescent signals in the night; the ladybugs and praying mantises whose ideas of a proper menu coincide with my list of insect enemies. The insects that I am aware of and can name (though not in Latin—I know only their common names, not scientific ones) make up only a tiny fraction of the insects and other creatures that inhabit the land I so foolishly tell myself I own. In his splendid book *The Secret Garden* (1992), David Bodanis reminds us that "The amount of life in even a tiny, half-inch-thick piece of soil from your lawn is difficult to grasp. There will be millions of miniature insects, and 5 billion or so bacteria—about as many as there are human beings on earth."

My ignorance of my garden is greater than what I do know, and whatever else I manage to learn during the rest of my days will be but a pittance, really.

Knowledge about plants adds to the pleasure of gardening, and it is clear that gardening is mental as well as physical exercise. But it's questionable whether any of the knowledge discussed in this chapter is truly essential. It may be highly desirable to make the effort to master botanical Latin, but it isn't absolutely necessary: hundreds of thousands of gardeners before and after Linneaus have gone happy to their graves without uttering a single Latin binomial. We can delight in regal lilies and grow them to perfection in our gardens without knowing anything about E. H. Wilson, his journeys to the Min Valley, and the lily limp he got from a landslide. Such knowledge deepens the pleasure that gardening brings; it is not essential knowledge.

Is there such essential knowledge in gardening? I believe that there is. The essence of gardening lies in caring for living beings, and it is impossible to care for anything that is alive without knowing what it needs in order to flourish.

Our planet offers an enormous diversity of habitats for both plants and animals. Temperature may be stable and well above freezing throughout the year, or there may be fierce, prolonged winters, sometimes followed by high heat and humidity in summer. Annual mean temperatures vary widely. Annual precipitation may be extremely high, very low, or anything in between. It may be evenly distributed during the year. It may be erratic, with long periods of drought broken by unpredictable heavy rain. It may be predictable but seasonal, as rainy seasons alternate with dry seasons. Soils may be alkaline or acidic in various degrees, or they may be neutral. They may be soggy and poorly aerated, moist but well drained, or parched and dry. Topsoil can be deep and rich in organic matter, or it may be thin and poor in organic matter. Some habitats are drenched in sunlight and swept by drying winds; some are deeply shaded and protected from wind by a dense forest canopy.

Every plant on earth has evolved to fit a particular niche within these wide diversities of conditions. You can't grow water lilies in desert sand, nor saguaro cactus in a swamp. You can't grow an orchid that evolved as an epiphyte (one that grows on trees) in garden soil, although you can grow terrestrial orchids there (provided that they are supplied with the fungi the plants need to survive for long).

Attempts to grow water lilies in sand or cactuses in swamps, of course, are extreme endeavors, and they are doomed quickly to extreme failure. Most other plants are more adaptable. They can survive, but never thrive, where conditions are uncongenial to their basic requirements. After all, if we can speak metaphorically of what plants "want"—of their system of desires, so to speak—their primary desire is to live, as a species if not as individuals. And even individual plants desire to keep on living. (We take advantage of this fierce determination to survive every time we take a cutting, which is a quite remarkable act, really. We cut from a plant a bit of stem and some leaves, severing it from the root system that provides it with moisture and nutrition. Cut off from its life-support system and given an environment where moisture is available, it may then proceed to develop roots, thus tending to its own survival in the face of considerable trauma.)

The art of gardening lies in part in knowing what plants need in order to thrive, not merely survive. I have seen gardens where the unhappy fact is immediately apparent that there is an unhappy marriage between the plants that grow there and the amount of light available to them. It may be a shady garden filled with light-loving plants, a place where roses, delphiniums, and culinary herbs languish in the gloom—a place made to order for ferns, hostas, pulmonarias, and other plants that find dim and shady nooks congenial. Conversely, it may be a sun-drenched garden where shade-loving plants suffer from excessive heat and light. It may be a dry garden, where moisture-hungry plants gasp and wilt as they struggle to survive. The love of plants that fills the heart of all true gardeners requires that we be attentive to their needs. Such attentiveness demands that we take pains to know their needs.

Love is the heart of the matter. We must learn what we need to know to care for the things we love.

CHAPTER 7

Larks and Angels

It rained yesterday, and a cold front just came through. Even though it's late July, the air is cool and fresh and the garden looks better than it sometimes does at this time of year, since the temperature has yet to reach above 90° F. and we haven't had more than five consecutive days without rainfall since early April. The garden is in full midsummer bloom, bright with lilies, hollyhocks, purple coneflowers and other daisies, and much else besides. But I'd like for now to single out two plants, each presently in full flower, and see how considering them leads out into a world far beyond this garden and all that can be known about it.

The first plant is *Corydalis flexuosa* 'Blue Panda', which has been blooming continuously since April. It is not the only corydalis in the garden, for *Corydalis lutea* has grown here for many years, self-seeding everywhere. The two resemble one another in several respects. Both have finely scalloped, dissected foliage that gives them an airy, delicate look. Both bear prolific crops of flowers over a long season stretching from mid-spring to late fall. Both have delicate racemes of flowers that in form are somewhat reminiscent of tiny birds—not surprising, since their genus name comes from the Greek *korydalis*, meaning "lark." But *C. lutea* bears yellow flowers and those of *C. flexuosa* 'Blue Panda' are blue, true blue—the blue of the sky on a cool crisp day, the blue of bluebirds—and they are diamond dusted with a white powdery overlay that sparkles in the light. If all that I knew about 'Blue Panda' were its name and what I could see before my

Plant collecting in East Asia continues into our own time, as is witnessed by the stately Angelica gigas *from Korea, first brought to America in 1985 by Barry Yinger and seen here at Heronswood Nursery in Kingston, Washington.*

eyes, I would be puzzled. Pandas aren't ever blue, are they? And even if they were, why should a plant with flowers like little birds be named for one? Let's hold off with the answer for a bit, in order to take up something else first.

Although 'Blue Panda' is very lovely up close, you could miss seeing it from some distance away. Not the other plant, for it is bold, dramatic, and impossible to overlook. Standing almost six feet tall and spreading nearly as much, it has just come into its two weeks of spectacular late summer bloom. Its green foliage is coarse in texture and deeply cut. The flower stems, which emerge from rounded and swollen leaf bracts of deep purple, bend at odd angles, like elbows or knees. The flowers are the most spectacular parts of this flamboyant plant. They are tiny, but there are a great many of them, arranged in clusters the size and shape of an orange cut in half. A lurid shade of purple verging on black, the clusters seem from a few feet away to throb and pulsate inexplicably. A closer look shows that a remarkable number of insects—flies, yellow jackets, blue wasps, and hornets—are lolling about on the flowers, languidly fanning their wings, resting as if intoxicated and unable to fly. The plant is *Angelica gigas*.

None of the books in my study help me find out more about either plant.

*T*he flowers of corydalis 'Blue
Panda' claim grace and charm, as
they perch like flocks of little birds
upon their stems. This recent import
from China brings to gardens a true
and very welcome shade of blue.

The New Royal Horticultural Society Dictionary of Gardening (1991), whose four volumes run to 3,240 pages, says nothing about either. It describes eight species of *Angelica,* forty-six of *Corydalis,* but not *A. gigas* and not *C. flexuosa.* From the dictionary and other books in my library I can learn something about the genus of each plant, and about some other species. The genus *Corydalis* is in the Poppy family. It is cosmopolitan, with species native to Europe, Asia Minor, East and West Asia, and North America. As for *Angelica,* in the Parsley family, it takes its name from angels, and the species most frequently grown, *Angelica archangelica,* is twice blessed or doubly divine. Its roots and seeds are used in flavoring liqueurs, and its candied stems are the angelica of bakeries and candy stores. In traditional medicine, this species of *Angelica* was believed to be effective in treating and preventing a variety of diseases and misfortunes, including the evil schemes of witches. In *The Herball* (1633), John Gerard wrote:

> The roots of garden Angelica are a singular remedy against poison, and against the plague, and all infections taken by evill and corrupt aire; if you but take a peece of the root and hold it in your mouth, or chew the same between your teeth, it doth most certainly drive away the pestilential aire, yea although that corrupt aire have possessed the hart, yet driveth it out again by urine and sweat. The root is available against witchcraft and inchantment, if a man carry it.

There is, incidentally, some chance that *Corydalis flexuosa* may have medical properties, like those that Gerard attributes to angelica. The Poppy family is rich in molecules of medical interest, such as the morphine and other drugs derived from the sap in the seed capsules of the opium poppy, *Papaver somniferum.* Furthermore, the powdered tubers of another species of *Corydalis, C. solida,* have long been used in traditional Chinese medicine as a sedative and painkiller.

As flowering plants, the corydalis and the angelica in my garden are both angiosperms, meaning that they evolved fairly recently. (The first angiosperms appeared roughly 114 million years ago.) *Angelica,* like *Corydalis,* is cosmopolitan in distribution—even more cosmopolitan, since the genus has a species native to New Zealand, as well as to Europe, Asia, and North America. The extremely wide range of geographical distribution of the two genera to which the plants growing in my garden belong suggests that each genus derives from a common ancestor that lived before the great landmasses began to break apart and go their separate ways. In this regard, they are like many other plants, such as hollies, oaks, pines, and beautyberries or callicarpas. As with these other plants, *Angelica gigas* and *Corydalis* 'Blue Panda' testify indirectly to the widely accepted theory of continental drift that was regarded as a crackpot idea as recently as the 1950s. (In 1952, when I asked the professor in a freshman geology class if it didn't strike him that some of the continents looked a bit like pieces of a jigsaw puzzle that fit together, he said, "Don't be absurd—this is a *science* class!" I love to think about the intellectual retooling he had to do!)

Considering that both of these plants obviously have a great deal of horticultural merit, it's logical to ask why *The New Royal Horticultural Society Dictionary* overlooks them. The answer is simple: these two plants are new in cultivation. *Angelica gigas* was collected from the wild in Korea in 1981, *Corydalis* 'Blue Panda' in China in 1986.

Here's the story of each.

Barry Yinger, an authority on East Asian plants who has collected a great many of them in their native habitats and introduced them to American gardens, tells me that he first encountered *Angelica gigas* during a three-day climb up Odae Mountain in northeastern Korea. On previous visits, he had been impressed by the rich flora of the mountain. "Odae," he says, "is one of the few areas in Korea that is in almost pristine condition, because of the protection afforded by the proximity of a number of Buddhist temples." Accompanied by Mr. Yong June Chang, a Korean friend, Yinger began to descend the mountain after reaching the top, taking a series of rough trails instead of following the most direct route. The two men arrived at an open, grassy area, surrounded by a forest of birches, maples, and magnolias. Here they found a diversity of herbaceous flora that Yinger describes as "astonishing"—five species of *Adenophora*, species of *Patrinia* in white and yellow, several species of *Aconitum* in shades of rich purple, blue, and creamy white, and the most elegant plant of all, *Hanabusaya asiatica*, "a Korean endemic with long, fluted, translucent bells of palest blue." Yinger then got his first sight of *Angelica gigas*, "towering above the splendid chaos all around." That fall, after he had returned to the United States, he received seeds that Yong June collected on Odae and planted them in his garden in Pennsylvania. The plants thrived, and they bloomed for the first time in 1983. Subsequently seeds were distributed through the U.S. National Arboretum, and plants were offered by such nurseries as Holbrook Farm (which is no longer in business), where I got the original plants from which those I now grow descended.

Yinger did not discover *Angelica gigas* in the sense that he was the first person ever to see it, nor did he give it its botanical name. It is described in Chang-Bok Lee's *Illustrated Flora of Korea.* The species name derives from Greek mythology, commemorating the race of humanlike beings of great strength and size who were destroyed after daring to battle the Olympian gods. Yinger muses that it "is strange that a plant so obvious should have escaped the attention of gardeners for such a long time, for its range is extensive, including Manchuria and the Kyushu and Shikoku Islands in Japan, as well as Korea." But he points out that it is uncommon in the wild, largely because of overcollecting for traditional Chinese medicine. One thing is certain, at any rate: without Barry Yinger's plant-hunting excursion back in 1981, this extraordinarily striking plant would not be in my garden today, throbbing with drunken insects.

'Blue Panda' is not the first blue-flowered corydalis to be discovered in East Asia by Western plant hunters. In *The Rainbow Bridge* (1926), a memoir of his expedition in China in 1914, the English explorer Reginald Farrer rhapsodized over a species he found there, *C. melanochlora.* The name seems to be invalid, but the point is not nomenclature but passion. Farrer wrote that among some "dumpy potentillas, the azure-blue Corydalis peered forth, in glints of turquoise. The elusiveness of love is nothing compared to that of Corydalis." Farrer was unsuccessful in gathering seed, and the copious number of tubers he brought back died after arrival, leaving him to lament that "*C. melanochlora* still waits introduction, on her gaunt scree—and it is well worth the pilgrimage, all for herself." Somewhat later, in *Plant Hunting on the Edge of the World* (1930), another Englishman, F. Kingdon Ward, describes a meadow in Assam "filled with thousands and thousands of small but brilliantly coloured flowers," including "a stunning blue Corydalis." There are other blue-flowered species of corydalis—*C. ambigua* from Japan, *C. cashmeriana* from the Himalayas, and others—but these are notoriously temperamental and difficult to grow. 'Blue Panda' is different, much easier to grow, although it may go dormant or perish utterly in late summer where summers are extremely hot and humid, and I once lost it by placing it in deep shade instead of the light shade it prefers.

'Blue Panda' is ordinarily described as a cultivar of *C. flexuosa*. But Rubin Hatch, the rhododendron specialist from Vancouver, Washington, who discovered it growing in huge colonies on the verges of woodlands in Sichuan, China, in early June of 1986, prefers to call it simply 'Blue Panda' ('Blue' because that's its color, 'Panda' because pandas live where it was found). Hatch wants to wait on the species name until a Swedish botanist who is working on the nomenclature of the genus, sorts everything out. Hatch's 'Blue Panda' isn't the only game in town when it comes to the genus. A year after he happened upon his prize, and 150 miles south of the Chinese woodland where he found it, the British plantsmen James Compton, John D'Arcy, and Martyn Rix collected three different forms of what they took to be unmistakably *C. flexuosa*. These were given the names 'China Blue', 'Pere David', and 'Purple Leaf'. All have blue flowers, and all are now available through such specialized nurseries as Heronswood, in Kingston, Washington. But 'Blue Panda' is by far the longest bloomer (although not where summers are hot and humid), and it has attracted the most attention. (A wholesale nursery in Oregon propagated 22,000 plants by tissue culture in 1996 and sold them all.)

Barry Yinger, Rubin Hatch, and other persons today who are exploring remote corners of the world to discover new plants and bring them home to enrich our gardens stand in an ancient tradition of plant hunting. This tradition begins in prehistoric times, with the domestication of cereal grains and other food crops and their subsequent dissemination from their native regions to other parts of the world. Let us launch out here on a summary examination of the history of this matter.

European and Middle Eastern agriculture came into being about 10,600 years ago when domesticated barley and wheat, different from their wild forms, appeared in Palestine. Gradually, over a period of some seven millennia, additional food crops—lentils, grapes, olives, alfalfa, and others—were domesticated. Independently, in other centers of civilization, agriculture also developed. Beans, potatoes, and sweet potatoes were domesticated in Peru 10,000 to 9,500 years ago, followed in time by maize in Mexico and sunflowers in northern North America. In Indonesia and New Guinea, beginning some 9,500 years ago, rice made its appearance, followed shortly by yams, sugarcane, bananas, coconuts, citrus fruits, and peaches. Later to appear were date palms, soybeans, and tea.

Plant domestication no sooner began than plants started traveling, with the importation of rice to Southern China from Southeast Asia some 9,000 years ago, and that of wheat and barley from the Middle East to Europe 8,500 years ago.

Even the most dedicated gardener will admit that food plants are much more important than purely ornamental ones. But flowers also went on the move as civilizations began to develop and to make connections with one another. In the Islamic world, garden plants like jasmines spread from Persia eastward to India and westward to Moorish Spain. In the Orient, many plants, such as chrysanthemums, were first grown in China and then imported to Japan. (Some scientific names using *japonica* as the species name—*Anemone japonica*, for example—are misleading, as the plants actually originated in China but made their way to the West from Japan.)

Soon after the European discovery of the New World, a new chapter began in the history of plant travels with human assistance. This explosion brought many new foodstuffs to the table as well as new ornamental plants to the garden. Initially, these novelties were brought back almost incidentally by Europeans whose interests were not primarily botanical, aesthetic, or culinary. Plant importers included the conquistadors—Hernán Cortés brought chocolate with him from Mexico on his return to Spain in 1519—and other explorers of new lands, merchant-traders, and missionaries.

I like to imagine what it would have been like to have lived in Europe several centuries ago, just as new plants were beginning to flood in from these new lands. I'm helped in this imaginative endeavor by two of the most treasured—and heaviest—books in my library, from which I've quoted several times already. They are facsimile editions of the greatest English herbals of the Renaissance, John Gerard's *The Herball: A Generall Historie of Plantes* (which was first published in 1597 and then revised and enlarged in 1633 by Thomas Johnson) and

In John Parkinson's vision of the earthly Eden, Adam and Eve tend a garden in which new plants from outside Europe, such as tulips from Asia Minor and pineapples from South America, grow alongside more familiar plants, such as calendulas and roses. [PARADISI IN SOLE]

John Parkinson's *Paradisi in Sole: Paradisus Terrestris* (1629). Written long before the world of plants had been tidied up by scientists, these herbals are a wondrous mix of miscellaneous knowledge and misinformation. Both Gerard and Parkinson gave their readers advice about what plants cure which diseases, or ease which discomforts. They struggled to describe plants with little in the way of the technical vocabulary capable of doing so clearly. They occasionally passed on, with entire seriousness, such utter nonsense as the plant Gerard describes at the very end of his herbal—a tree that bears barnacles that in due course turn into geese. (The most embarrassing thing about this aberration is that Gerard claims to have seen it with his own eyes, touched it with his own hands.)

What is most fascinating in the writings of these classic British herbalists is that they were writing at a time when a massive importation of new plants into

One page from Paradisi in Sole *accurately renders a number of New World plants, such as daturas and flowering tobacco. At lower right appears one of Parkinson's particular favorites, the marvel of Peru or the four o'clock. [*PARADISI IN SOLE*]*

Europe was just getting under way. Europeans ventured outward into the rest of the world after 1492, starting with the conquest of Mexico in 1519–1521 and Peru in 1531–1533. The conquistadors and missionaries brought home from their journeys seeds of plants that Europeans had never seen before. Tulips and lilacs arrived in England by the early 1580s, possibly earlier. The comparatively meager native English flora was beginning to be greatly enlarged by the importation of plants in a process that continues to this day. Gerard and later Parkinson both had many new plants to write about.

John Gerard could already see in his own garden the new plants from outlandish places that his grandfather and his father never knew. But it is fascinating to wonder what he would think if he had fallen into a Rip Van Winkle sleep in 1597, the year the first edition of his book came out, and not awakened until

No geographical purist, Cynthia Woodyard arranges wonderful plant marriages—and polygamous ones at that—among plants from all the world's temperate zones .

Asiatic lilies, Eurasian Clematis integrifolia, European yarrow, Verbascum chaixii (native to Europe from Spain to Poland), and a hybrid rose called 'Eye Paint' mingle together to grand and opulent effect.

Regal lilies from China, agapanthus from South Africa, and an unusually early-blooming species of goldenrod from North America hold down the center of this richly complex grouping of plants.

In this plant ménage, spikiness is the theme, as verbascums, the campanula 'Loddon's Anna', and Stachys macrantha *vie with one another in their steepling ambitions.*

our own time, four centuries later. He would have awakened to gardens filled with startlingly unfamiliar plants. There might still be the English primroses (*Primula vulgaris*) that he loved, but they would grow alongside *P. capitata, P. obconica,* and *P. vialii*—other species of primrose from the Himalayas and China, in colors and forms he would find unimaginably strange. He would see familiar European madonna lilies, damask roses, and ferny-leafed little peonies, but he would also see new Asian species within the genera *Lilium, Rosa,* and *Paeonia,* as well as hybrids between them and European species. Azaleas, cacti, camellias, dahlias, and magnolias would all amaze him. I'm sure he would have enjoyed a blue corydalis to match the yellow one he knew. His jaw would probably drop at the sight of a purple angelica throbbing with stinging and biting fauna.

With the establishment of European colonies in the Americas, plants moved in both directions between the Old World and the New. Sometimes the exchange was accidental, as when European weeds like dandelion and plantain weed came to the North America in ships' ballast. Sometimes it was intentional. The English settlers who came to New England and Virginia sent for the familiar garden plants of their homeland. Many of these, like bouncing bet and queen anne's lace, escaped from colonial gardens to naturalize in American fields and woodland edges. By 1620, gardens in Massachusetts included European grapes, wheat, rye, potatoes, barley, oats, hops, apple and other fruit trees, parsley, sage, flax, turnips, cucumbers, onions, and muskmelons. Carnations, European species of columbine, hollyhocks, lilies, primroses, tulips, and many herbs were soon thereafter part of American gardens. There was also great and increasing interest in Europe in native American flora.

The earliest stage of this two-way traffic between England and its North American colonies is an exercise in anonymity, but in time names came to be attached to human-driven plant migration. John Tradescant the Younger (1608–1662) made three trips to Virginia in 1637, 1647, and 1654, returning to England with seeds of many native North American plants. One of them—*Tradescantia virginiana,* a spiderwort—is named for his family. A good bit later (1712–1714), another Englishman, Mark Catesby (1679–1749), began collecting American plants for English consumption during a stay in Virginia. Among the North American plants he introduced to England were *Catalpa bignon-*

ioides, Magnolia grandiflora, and *Stewartia malacodendron.* Plantsmen born in America also figured in the story. John Bartram (1699–1777), one of several "Quaker botanists" who worked in Philadelphia, collected over 200 species of North American plants to send to England. His son William (1739–1823) traveled extensively through the southeastern United States, collecting plants and observing wildlife, southern customs, and American Indians. His *Travels through North and South Carolina, Georgia, and East and West Florida* (1792) is one of the classic (and still highly readable) texts of plant exploration. The plant most closely associated with his name is the lovely shrub *Franklinia alatamaha,* a member of the Tea family with single, creamy white camellia-like flowers in the fall, when it also develops beautiful bronze-red leaves. Bartram discovered it in Georgia, near the Alatamaha River. Named for Benjamin Franklin, it was never again found growing in the wild. It is likely that he located it just as it was on the very brink of extinction—a lucky event, for it is one of the most beautiful of all American woody plants.

The French-born André Michaux (1746–1802) collected seeds of many useful and beautiful plants in Persia from 1782 through 1785, when the king of France sent him to the New World as king's botanist. He established nurseries in Bergen County, New Jersey, and Charleston, South Carolina. Before returning to France in 1796 he introduced to American gardens mimosa trees, camellias, indica azaleas, ginkgos, chinaberries, crape myrtles, and many other woody plants that are still of great importance, especially in the South. Among the plants he introduced to Europe were Catawba rhododendrons, several North American native azaleas, Carolina jessamine, yucca, magnolias, and junipers.

Although George Washington was no mean gardener and farmer himself, the palm of honor goes to Thomas Jefferson (1743–1826) as the greatest gardener, farmer, and botanical enthusiast ever to be chief of state in any nation. During his diplomatic travels in England and Europe before he became our third president, Jefferson observed gardens and plants, keeping records which remain lively and fascinating reading. He illegally gathered grains of a superior Italian strain of rice and smuggled them home, where they became a staple economic crop in South Carolina's Low Country. He tried (unsuccessfully) to grow oranges at Monticello, his Virginia home, and he sent seeds of many American plants, such as pecan and sweet gum, to England and France. He organized the

Lewis and Clark expedition to the Pacific Northwest, partly to establish U.S. territorial claims to the land and partly to bring back useful or ornamental species of plants from the region of the Missouri River and westwards.

The primary means for the transportation of plants from one place to another was through seeds, although some living plants were taken across the Atlantic. Plants also were pressed, dried, and preserved as specimens for the herbariums often associated with botanical gardens.

Contrary to what many seem to believe today, gardens are not English inventions, and scientific botany has been an international pursuit since its beginning. But in the nineteenth century Great Britain did play a major role, in the great ingathering of plants, especially from the tropics, for several reasons. First, gardening in England was a gentlemanly occupation, taken seriously by wealthy and powerful patrons willing to underwrite expeditions to bring back rare and exotic plants from faraway places. Nurseries were also eager to obtain new plants for their customers. Scientific societies and institutions with royal backing wanted to be major players in the business of plant collecting. Botanical magazines thrived, as did gardening books. Second, England has a gentler climate than most of North America, even though it is at the same latitude as Labrador. Courtesy of the Gulf Stream, its winters can be gray and bleak but are seldom fiercely cold. Thanks to its high latitude its summers are cool, with long days and short nights. This blessed climate makes outdoor gardening with sometimes temperamental plants something Americans, especially those who lust after delphiniums, can only dream about.

Because most of the former British colonies were in tropical and subtropical regions around the equator, British colonial governors became familiar with the often fantastic flora of the tropics. Their reports of what they saw in these parts of the world excited the acquisitive instincts of their countrymen back home, who were in any case daft for the new, the rare, and the exotic (and probably bored with English primroses). Unfortunately, there were grave technical obstacles to bringing tropical plants to England. On the long sea journey, plants kept in the holds of ships died for want of light and those on deck perished from salt water and exposure. The seeds of tropical plants are often fleshy and very perishable. Even if some plants survived the trip or their seeds remained viable, they then faced England's winter—mild, but still something which almost no plants that evolved in frost-free parts of the world could survive. All of these obstacles were finally overcome, in a tale whose greatest heroes are glass and steam.

In 1827 Dr. Nathaniel Bagshaw Ward (1791–1868), a somewhat absent-minded London physician and passionate amateur entomologist, put a caterpillar in a glass jar to pupate, sealed the jar with a stopper, and then forgot about it. Later he discovered small plants growing inside the jar, because of the moisture that evaporated, condensed on its walls and then fell back, in a repeated cycle. This chance discovery led to Ward's invention of the terrarium, a closed system of glass, plants, and constantly recycling moisture. Ward's terrarium, which he described in *On the Growth of Plants in Closely Glazed Cases* (1842), was quickly adapted by plant collectors in the form of Wardian cases, large-scale terrariums that were widely used to ship vast numbers of species of tropical and subtropical plants to England.

Glass is one of the most ancient of man-made materials, but the glass Ward used was the product of a new technology in which it was manufactured in thin sheets that let light through while retaining moisture and, to some extent, heat. Cut into panes, this glass—once combined with steam—could also be used in greenhouses and conservatories for growing tropical plants in the north temperate zone. The use of steam as a source of heat enabled coal-fired furnaces, whose noxious fumes kill plants, to transmit their heat from a safe distance through simple systems of pipes and flues. Combining glass and steam heat meant that tropical conditions of heat and humidity could be imitated indoors, if not reproduced exactly. Thus developed the great greenhouses or conservatories that were the architectural symbols of the Victorian age.

Despite the importance of glass and steam, the continuing story of plant exploration in exotic locales for the gardens and greenhouses closer to home remains primarily a human story. Much of this story is British, since the British have been particularly keen at keeping track of the history of their dealings with plants. I will here content myself with only one of the important nineteenth-century British plant hunters, Robert Fortune (1813–1880), because his plant discoveries in eastern Asia brought us such a great number of by-now-familiar and well-loved plants. The first collector to use the Wardian case, Fortune made enormous contributions to Western gardening through the many plants he collected in China and Japan. His four journeys to the Far East gave us *Anemone japonica, Dicentra spectabilis,* and *Mahonia lomariifolia.* Our winter gardens would be bleaker without the shining evergreen foliage of his *Aucuba japonica* and the bright yellow flowers of his winter jasmine (*Jasminum nudiflorum*).

We have, of course, already considered Ernest H. Wilson, who brought us regal lilies from the Min Valley, at great peril to his life.

In our own day, the search for new plants continues, particularly in East Asia, at the accelerated pace made possible by jet travel. This part of the world has been something of a jackpot for Western plant explorers for two hundred years, and new finds, such as corydalis 'Blue Panda' and *Angelica gigas,* are still being made. (The flora of this region and that of North America are extremely rich in comparison with that of Europe. It's a matter of geology and glaciation. Mountain ranges in Europe run east and west, those in East Asia and North America north and south. The difference in orientation means that when glaciers begin to spread south during an Ice Age, plants have no escape in Europe, as they do where mountains and valleys run north and south. Orientation

Robert Fortune brought to Western gardens many choice plants from East Asia, such as bleeding heart. [JOURNAL OF HORTICULTURE, COTTAGE GARDENER, *and* HOME FARMER III, VOL. 38, 1989. COURTESY OF THE PHOTOGRAPHIC ARCHIVES OF THE ARNOLD ARBORETUM]

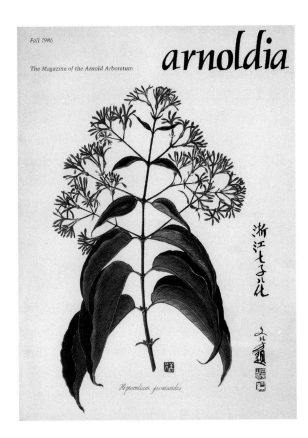

Fall 1986

The Magazine of the Arnold Arboretum

arnoldia

One of the most recent plants *from China to enrich our gardens,* Heptacodium miconioides *is notable for the rich perfume of it flowers in autumn.*
[PHOTOGRAPHIC ARCHIVES OF
THE ARNOLD ARBORETUM]

Heptacodium jasminoides

brings about extinction of species in the former case, survival in the second.) As I walk around my garden, I can identify a number of Asian plants that were unknown in Western gardens in 1935, when I was born.

One of the handsomest of these is my tallest tree, at fifty feet, a twenty-five-year-old dawn redwood (*Metasequoia glyptostroboides*), a living fossil if ever there was one. Thought to have been extinct, it turned up in a remote area of China in 1941. In 1948 seeds were sent to the Arnold Arboretum, which was responsible for its introduction. Like the bald cypress, which it somewhat resembles, it is a deciduous conifer. It is beautiful in every season, from the time its delicate, feathery, pale-green leaves appear in early spring until its foliage turns a luscious apricot with strawberry overtones in fall; the red-brown exfoliating bark on its massive bole is lovely in winter.

There are other East Asian plants, newcomers to my garden, that have great merit. One is *Heptacodium miconioides,* a rarity even in its native China but already becoming popular among American gardeners since its arrival here in 1980. A small tree, to about twenty feet, it produces clusters of tiny, jasmine-scented flowers in September, followed by showy red-purple bracts that remain attractive for weeks afterward. (The tree seems to bloom twice—first white, then red.) The foliage is a choice glossy green, and the exfoliating bark lends the plant interest in winter. Then there's *Lagerstroemia fauriei,* a crape myrtle, also with exfoliating bark, and considerably more winter-hardy than the more familiar cultivars of *Lagerstroemia indica* that are so glorious for most of the summer in the South. Hybrids between the two species are making it possible to extend the range of crape myrtles into colder regions of the United States.

There are still other worthy new Asian immigrants. A newly collected Korean form of *Campsis grandiflora,* the Chinese trumpet vine, produces huge pinkish apricot flowers for months, and it is reliably winter-hardy to at least to Zone 6, unlike forms previously collected in southern China. *Styrax japonicum* 'Carillon' is a small tree offering pendant branches bearing large white flowers shaped like chalices. *Loropetalum chinense* var. *rubrum* has lovely, wispy pink flowers over a long season, borne above contrasting foliage of smoky purple. It is not sufficiently winter-hardy that I can grow it in southern New Jersey with complete confidence, but it has rapidly become extremely popular with southern gardeners. Finally, in this much abbreviated catalog of the Asian plants that will be very prominent in American gardens in the twenty-first century, I should mention *Vitex rotundifolia,* which was collected by T. R. Dudley, Barry Yinger, and the late J. C. Raulston in a U.S. National Arboretum plant exploration expedition to the southwest coast and islands of the Republic of Korea in 1985. A low, spreading shrub with silvery-blue leaves and blue flowers, this vitex was found growing right next to the ocean's edge, making it potentially a highly valuable plant for seaside gardens.

Plant collectors have recently been busy in the Southwest and in the mountains of northern Mexico, as well as in Japan, Korea, and China. European plant explorers were active in an area stretching from Texas to Southern California, bringing home with them a great many of our native plants, particularly such annuals as California poppy and Drummond's phlox. The region is now being mined by American horticulturists and nurserymen who seek out, in particular, herbaceous plants with a high degree of drought tolerance, such as a number of different species of *Agastache, Penstemon,* and *Tagetes.*

I have mentioned salvias already, but the really good news about this marvelous genus is that recent explorations in the mountains of northern Mexico, primarily under the auspices of Yucca-Do Nursery in Texas, have turned up several terrific species, such as the shrubby, late-blooming *Salvia mexicana.* No doubt more species are to come, as this part of North America has largely been neglected by plant hunters until very recently.

New plants do not remain new for long. Those that are especially choice can move with surprising speed to garden centers across the country from botanical gardens, arboretums, and small nurseries specializing in rarities. Yesterday's novelties may become tomorrow's staples, and the rare may sooner or later become commonplace and familiar. But searching for new and garden-worthy plants is an ongoing affair, to the extent that we may be confident that gardeners a generation—even several generations—yet to come will long for plants whose existence we cannot even dream of, and that they will feel grateful to the adventurous plant explorers and collectors who will have sought them out in the four corners of the world.

Of late there's been a minor skirmish in American gardening between those who advocate the widest possible, possibly exclusive, use of our native plants, and those who feel that it would be extremely unwise to deprive ourselves of exotics, such as those from East Asia. I understand the arguments of the native-plant partisans. For one thing, some of the most troublesome plants in our landscapes are exotics, including those that have escaped from gardens into the wild. (Think crabgrass, honeysuckle, kudzu!) The native vegetation of our eastern and midwestern wetlands is suffering badly from the invasive ways of the European purple loosestrife (*Lythrum salicaria*). In the Deep South, water hyacinths clog streams, canals, and rivers, costing millions of dollars annually to attempt to control. The list of takeover plants that plague Florida, such as Australian "pine" (*Casuarina equisetifolia*), is daunting in size. Other malefactors there include the Brazilian pepper tree, *Schinus terebinthifolius,* introduced in the 1890s, and the Australian cajeput tree, *Melaleuca quinquenervia,* which was deliberately set loose in 1906 by a land developer with some training in forestry, but not enough. Both plants compete too successfully with native shrubs and trees, and also cause painful skin rashes in susceptible persons.

Such examples signal the need for caution in regard to exotic plants, but I cannot agree with the proposition that exotic species should be drummed out of our gardens in favor of supposedly superior North American species—a chauvinistic assumption that makes little horticultural sense. The native American fringe tree, *Chionanthus virginicus,* is subject to blight, but the Chinese species, *C. retusus,* is not; the eastern dogwod, *Cornus florida,* is suffering damage from drought and disease throughout much of its range, but the Chinese dogwood, *C. kousa,* is so far unscathed—and moreover has produced hybrids with *C. florida* that carry its genes for resistance to disease. There are many such cautionary examples evidencing the need to restrain undue notions that native necessarily means better. We should, after all, consider the fate of the American chestnut and the American elm and their virtual extermination when chestnut blight and Dutch elm disease came along.

Besides, I like the idea of a garden as a United Nations, where plants from all over the world grow alongside one another in perfect harmony—where Asian peonies consort with Turkish tulips and American phloxes, and dawn redwoods from China look down on Virginia bluebells from our eastern woodlands. I like to think of all the plant explorers past and present who have suffered inconveniences and hardships and sometimes risked their lives in order that we might all garden—and garden more abundantly.

CHAPTER 8

What the Daisies Tell

It's another summer afternoon in my pursuit of what gardening gives the mind to chew on, and we have company. A friend has dropped by for iced coffee, together with her children, a girl of seven, and a boy and a girl, who are twins of four. They are playing quietly in the back garden, beyond the deck where we sit in the shade of the hardy kiwi vine on the pergola. The boy is walking slowly about the lawn, head down as if in deep study. The seven-year-old asked if she could pick a flower. I said yes, and she picked a daisy. Now she is huddled together with the younger girl, whispering something as she pulls off the petals one by one. I can't hear what she is saying, but I know: she is initiating her sister into the ritual whereby daisies are supposed to tell us what we wish to know. Her brother, I'm pretty sure, is looking for a four-leaf clover.

The long history of gardening and of our transactions with the world of plants is chock-full of old, discredited knowledge, of "truths" that were once solemnly believed but have now lost almost all standing. *Plants can foretell the future. They can bring us good fortune. They have a special significance in our dreams. They carry out transactions with gods. They have meanings, just as words do.* Even though such ideas no longer have currency, they are worth some exploration, for they are part of our own intellectual history. They are the things we used to think but have abandoned along the way.

Some people still believe that finding a four-leaf clover brings good luck, that we can tell our loves by plucking off the ray flowers of a daisy one by one while reciting "She loves me, She loves me not," and that in the Christmas season we must kiss anyone standing under a sprig of mistletoe. These and a few other such ideas are still being passed on from one generation to the next, but many more are now found only in books of curiosities—or have passed into oblivion.

Before we meet our mates, it is natural for us to feel some curiosity. Will they be ugly or handsome or somewhere in between? Will they be dark or fair, blue-eyed or brown-eyed? We know that there is no way of answering such questions in advance. But as late as the opening years of our century, young women in country districts of England thought they had an infallible means of discovering who their husbands would be. A young woman would gather nine holly leaves, as free of prickles as she could find, put them in a three-cornered handkerchief, tie it with nine knots, put it under her pillow, and then go to sleep. All of these things had to be done on a Friday. If the instructions were followed exactly, she would dream about her husband-to-be.

Other ancient English lore held that anyone who was sick would surely die if holly was brought inside the house before Christmas Eve. It was also unlucky to leave holly indoors past Shrove Tuesday, when it had to be burned in a fire on which pancakes were cooked. By contrast, if holly had previously been used to decorate a church, a sprig could always be brought home, and it would invariably bring good fortune to all who lived there.

Dreaming about plants could foretell our futures. If we dreamed of a boxwood hedge when we were young, we knew that we would live long and prosperous lives amidst an uncommonly happy family. If we dreamed instead of a yew, an aged relative we had never met or known would die soon, bequeathing to us a great fortune. (But one should never fall asleep under a yew, for to do so was thought to be lethal.)

Today, such lore about plants is rare to the vanishing point. It would be encouraging to think that these notions have virtually departed from our consciousness because they are superstitious and because superstition has vanished from our midst. But in truth, I see little evidence that the day of superstition is over. (I have a number of friends who contrive never to leave a house through a door different from the one they came in. I know someone with a doctorate in political science from Harvard who buries his nail parings, lest someone find them and put a curse on him by cursing his discarded fingernail clippings. I am not entirely free of something similar. By reflex action, I still throw a pinch of salt over my shoulder if I spill some at the table.) I attribute the death of plant lore not to the death of superstition but to the homogeneity of a culture that has forgotten what is local and quirky, giving us instead the icons of television and the movies.

In a dry spot along the driveway, periwinkles are blooming, not the *Vinca minor* and *V. major* that bloom in early spring, but the tropical perennials that are grown as annuals in temperate regions. Once *Vinca rosea,* they have been put in their own genus, as *Catharanthus roseus.* When summer arrives for sure and the heat cranks up, they are splendid plants, able to survive drought and attractive for their glossy, deep green foliage and their generous flowering over a long season, when they bear blossoms of pure white, deep rose, or white with a rosy-red eye. They aren't subject to any diseases, and insects won't touch them, for these plants, native to Madagascar, are loaded with highly toxic alkaloids. It's a good thing, too. Twenty-five years ago, Hodgkin's disease was fatal 90 percent of the time. Now there's a recovery rate of about 80 percent, as a result of vincristine and vinblastine, drugs based on the molecules found in the alkaloids *Catharanthus roseus* produces for its own defense against predators.

Despite the profound differences between modern Western medicine and medicine as it was practiced in earlier times, both agree that some plants have curative powers. A high percentage—40 percent or more—of the drugs and medications found in pharmacies today either derive directly from plants or contain molecules synthesized to mimic those found naturally in certain plants. Aspirin, belladonna, digitalis, morphine and related compounds, quinine, reserpine—we possess all of these and other drugs only because they or their analogues were first manufactured not in a laboratory but in the living cells of plants. Some contraceptives originated in chemical experiments with a wild Mexican yam, and the seeds of at least one species of evening primrose contain gamma-linolenic acid, a drug useful in treating arthritis and heart disease.

Plants vary enormously in their chemistry and in their power to help cure our diseases and heal our wounds. Many plants are toxic, even lethal, in whole or in part; many others are neither harmful nor helpful. Sorting out their medical properties has been a long and continuous process of trial and error. It would be enormously helpful if we could just look at a plant and find clues about whether it would benefit us or not. That simply doesn't seem to be the case, but some human beings once thought otherwise. During the Middle Ages, belief grew up in something called the doctrine of signatures. According to this doctrine, God not only created certain plants for the express purpose of curing and healing us but also gave us hints about their uses. A plant with heart-shaped leaves would be useful in treating coronary disease. Kidney-shaped leaves were signs that the plant bearing them provided medicine for renal ailments. These beliefs had a long run, but they were based on the assumption that human beings stood at the center of all creation, able to decipher the messages to us that it contained.

We know better now. But we can still be grateful for the curative powers that turn out to lie in those periwinkles that grow along our driveway.

Many years ago I planted a few pips of lily of the valley under a little white pine at a far corner of the garden, thinking it would be a fine thing to be able to pick bouquets of their stems with their nodding white bells of flowers in the spring. The flowers have a fresh sweet scent, and they seem somehow shy and demure, since they point downward, as if not wishing to be looked in the eye. The pine has now grown immense, and the lily of the valley turns out to be far from shy. It spreads slowly, but it spreads relentlessly, pushing aside everything in its path, except of course for the white pine. I now know I must do something to halt its advance. I should have known better than to plant it to begin with, of course. Southern New Jersey has many acres of farmland that has reverted to pine woodlands. The farmhouses collapsed long ago, little remaining of them now but their brick foundations. The women of these farms planted lily of the valley next to their houses. It now spreads in vast colonies far into the woods. Lily of the valley does quiet battle with other vegetation—and it wins.

I am not the first to associate this plant with conflict and victory. According to Christian lore, the lily of the valley originated as the result of a fierce battle between saintliness and wickedness. Saint Leonard went to the woods to live as a hermit, communing with God in his every waking moment. A dragon named Temptation, who lived in the woods, resented the saint's presence. After the dragon went to Leonard's hut and burned it down with his fiery breath, the two fought a mighty three-day battle before the dragon was slain. Every drop of dragon blood turned into a poisonous weed; every drop of Leonard's blood became a lily of the valley. (Never mind that lilies of the valley are highly poisonous!)

This story fits a pattern. Both classical and Christian mythology abound in stories telling how particular plants came into existence as a result of the actions of gods, demigods, heroes, and saints. The most familiar of these stories involves the handsome youth named Narcissus, with whom Echo, a mountain nymph, fell in love. Hers was an unfortunate choice, because Narcissus spent all his time gazing at his own reflection in a pool of water. The spurned Echo finally faded away, leaving behind nothing but her voice. The gods, angered by Narcissus's self-involvement and vanity, turned him into a flower, destined always to sit by a pool nodding at his own reflected image.

The peony has a similar legendary origin. Paeon was physician to the gods and a student of Asclepius, the god of medicine. Leto, the goddess of fertility, told Paeon about a magical root growing on Mount Olympus that would soothe the pains of childbirth. When Paeon got the root, Asclepius flew into a jealous rage and tried to kill his pupil. Paeon was rescued by Zeus, who turned him into a flower.

Of all plants, none has accumulated more legends than the rose. According to Greek mythology, when Aphrodite was born from the sea foam of the Mediterranean, all roses were white. But when Adonis, her handsome lover, was fatally wounded by a boar while hunting, his blood fell on a rose and stained it. Ever since, the roses descended from the rose of Adonis have been red. A rival story, from Roman mythology, holds that Cupid, the son of Venus (Aphrodite in Roman dress), gave us red roses when, intoxicated on wine, he spilled some on a rose. Later, angered when a bee stung him as he was sniffing a rose, Cupid shot the plant with an arrow. Roses, ever since, have borne thorns.

Pagan mythology did not vanish with the advent of Christianity. Instead, it was transformed. By the fourth century A.D., Saint Ambrose asserted that red roses symbolized the blood of martyrs and that their thorns were emblematic of early Christian sufferings. He also held that roses alone among flowers originated not on earth but in heaven, where they bore no thorns. At the moment when Adam and Eve sinned in the garden of paradise, the rose fell from heaven and was equipped with stabbing thorns to remind us of our transgressions. The beauty and fragrance of the blossoms, however, remained as divine signs of our hope of salvation and of the heavenly paradise to come.

Roses are also associated with Christ. Saint Bernard of Clairvaux held that the five petals of the sweetbrier or eglantine (*Rosa rubiginosa*) represented the five wounds of Christ—the spear to his side and the nails piercing his hands and feet. In another symbolic interpretation, the sweetbrier's petals stood for Christ's five senses. The scholastic theologian Albertus Magnus taught that all roses were white until the crucifixion, when the blood of Christ stained some red as a sign of redemption. A parallel legend held that the crown of thorns was fashioned from the stems of roses stripped of their flowers—as opposed to the crowns of the Caesars, made of rose blossoms with their stems stripped of thorns.

The Virgin Mary was even more closely associated with roses than Christ in the Marian piety that developed during medieval times. Mary was considered "a rose without thorns," because the immaculate conception kept her pure of the original sin that taints all other human beings. White roses stood for her freedom from sin, red ones for her sorrows during the crucifixion.

At one time, many of the plants that we grow in our gardens were believed to have theological meaning, to testify to us about the gods. They were sermons not expressed in words. The stories now exist only in books and libraries, not as living elements of our imaginations. But that these stories were once preached to us lends an added dimension to our delight in roses or our observation that once lilies of the valley begin to do battle, they always win.

If we have a quarrel with someone we love and are sorry and wish to make things right again, we may call up a florist and ask that flowers be sent. Or we may pick a bouquet from our garden and deliver it ourselves. The flowers symbolize our desire to apologize and our hope to be forgiven. We give the flowers their symbolic meaning, and it is understood, but they have no intrinsic meaning all their own, independent of our intent.

It was not always so. Well into modern times, the idea that plants meant something was highly prevalent.

The notion that specific flowers have symbolic meanings, so that human beings—lovers particularly—might communicate with each other by sending a bouquet or an individual flower, came into Western European thinking with two travelers to Turkey who wrote about the sélam, a kind of love letter composed of objects (which might include flowers, without being restricted to them). In 1718, Lady Mary Montagu wrote of this Turkish custom: "There is no colour, no flower, no weed, no fruit, herb, pebble, or feather that has not a verse belonging to it; and you may quarrel, reproach, or send Letters of passion, friendship, or Civility, or even of news, without ever inking your fingers." She went on to describe one such sélam as composed of a clove, a jonquil, a lump of coal, a rose, a grape, and a straw—but didn't translate its meaning. In *Voyages du Sr. A. De La Mottraye en Europe, en Asie et en Afrique* (1727), Aubrey De La Mottraye, who had visited Charles XII of Sweden in his exile in Turkey, not only described a sélam but also explained its meaning. A pear, a clod of earth, some honey, a feather, an onion, a piece of thread, and a jujube—these sent from a woman to a man meant "Don't be afraid nor give up hope. Once you abandon all your other lovers, I will be yours—and your slave in bed."

The major figure in the further development of the notion of a language of flowers, however, was Charlotte De La Tour (a pseudonym for someone whose identity has remained utterly mysterious), who published *Le Langage des Fleurs* in 1819, remarking that one of her purposes was to help readers "write a letter or compose a sélam." But in her system of communication flowers were the only vocabulary; gone were the honey and the straw. For De La Tour, the daffodil meant "false hope." Daturas signified "deceitful charms," and red geraniums "folly." *Le Langage des Fleurs* was translated into German in 1820 and into English in 1834, initiating a flood of similar books that became best-sellers. The genre abounded in plagiarism, as writer after writer cribbed from others to explain that a pimpernel symbolized "change" (but also "assignation") and a pineapple stood for "you are perfect." Roses, as may be imagined, figured especially in these dictionaries of floral sentiments. Mrs. Sarah Josepha Hale's *Flora's Interpreter and Fortuna Flora,* published in Boston in 1858, explained that burgundy roses meant "simplicity and beauty." Fresh white roses expressed "sadness," but if wilted, they signified "despair." A yellow rose meant "let us forget." (Mrs. Hale wasn't specific about what it was that needed to be forgotten, but another book, also published in Boston in 1858, Catherine H. Waterman's *Flora's Lexicon,* spelled it out: a yellow rose said, "You have been unfaithful to me, and I know it.")

In this supposed language, flowers were the words, but there was also a grammar, provided by human gestures. The meaning of a flower was reversed if it was presented upside down; a salvia that right side up meant "I esteem you" meant the opposite if reversed. Meaning also altered if a flower was given with the left hand, not the right: the left hand implied insincere sentiment.

The idea that there could be a language of flowers, that the daffodil or the lily had some intrinsic meaning, was the highly sentimentalized dying gasp of an ancient misunderstanding of the relationship between humans and the plant kingdom. From the time of the Greek gods and of the Middle Eastern vegetation demigods like Adonis or Dionysus up until the mid-nineteenth century, it was possible to believe that plants had meanings. When Charles Darwin published *On the Origin of Species* in 1859—a year after Mrs. Hale's *Flora's Interpreter*—the game was up. Plants could still say things, but only in the literature of pure fancy, as in Lewis Carroll's *Through the Looking-Glass* (1871):

> "O Tiger-lily," said Alice, addressing herself to one that was waving gracefully about in the wind, "I *wish* you could talk!"
>
> "We *can* talk," said the Tiger-lily: "when there's anybody worth talking to."

In the conversation among the plants in this talking garden, the Rose thinks that Alice's face "has some sense in it, though it's not a clever one," then grants that "it's the right color, and that goes a long way." (Alice has rosy cheeks.) The Tiger-lily rejoins that he doesn't care about the color, but that Alice's "petals" need to curl up a little more. There is a great deal of amusing intellectual nonsense in this passage: trees "bark," and of course say "bough-wough" when they do, and the Tiger-lily explains to Alice that she's never heard plants talk in other gardens because their beds are so soft that the flowers are always asleep. But there's also a philosophical dead hit on the anthropomorphism with which human culture before the dawn of the age of science has regarded plants, trying to pull them into our orbit of meanings. To do so is to fail to understand what they really are. If flowers could think and speak about us, Carroll suggests, they would get it all wrong, just as we long did about them.

Plants do send messages, of course, but not to human beings and in no human language. Flowering plants, except those that depend on the wind for pollination, announce themselves to their pollinators in the visual language of color and in the chemical language of smell. When we look admiringly at a flower or delight in its scent we look only with our own two human eyes. We have no idea whatsoever what it looks like to a honeybee, with its more than 12,000 visual lenses, in a set of five eyes—two compound and three simple—that are capable of perceiving the ultraviolet light that we cannot and incapable of perceiving the red light that we can. Looking at a primrose that seems to us solid yellow, we do not see the markings visible in ultraviolet light that show a bee the way to its nectary and its stamens and pistil. Similarly, the fragrance of flowers may so please us that we may gather nosegays, distill their essences in substances used in perfumes and in cooking, and associate them with our deepest and most powerful memories and desires. But again, as we have seen already, we are olfactory eavesdroppers.

Plants also send messages, we are learning of late, to other plants. An oak tree under attack by predators, such as a plague of gypsy moths, alters its chemistry to produce repellent toxic compounds. Through some means, perhaps atmospheric gases, other nearby trees, not yet under attack, begin the same chemical defense. The exact mechanisms through which such extraordinary transactions occur are by no means fully understood, but it is undeniable that they do occur. We have believed much nonsense about plants, but the truths about them can be much stranger than any of our imaginings.

From the mid-nineteenth century right up to the present, it has been increasingly difficult, if not impossible, to put any stock at all in the notion that plants move in our orbit of meanings and symbols. Our lives—the lives of all animals in fact—depend on them, but they have nothing to say to us.

Curiously, belief to the contrary is invincible in some quarters. Some extremely strange ideas about plants still get a hearing. *Plants have emotional lives,* we are told. *They fear people who would do them harm*—or who have a history of mistreating other plants. *They get lonely:* sometimes a rubber plant taken to the lobby of a bank from the greenhouse where it grew with others of its kind will sicken and die because it misses its old companions. Plants *hear, remember,* and *can count as high as twenty. They respond to music,* although not as favorably to rock music as to Mozart and Bach. Music, it has been asserted, can alter the chromosome counts of plants. Plants *sympathize with the suffering of others,* even others not of their kind: if living brine shrimp are plunged into boiling water nearby, while plants are hooked up to a polygraph, a wild fluttering of the instrument's needles shows their emotional distress.

Little of this is strange, were we considering ourselves. We fear those who harm us, or who have harmed others. We feel lonely when we are deprived of companionship. We delight in music. We are upset when other living things suffer . . . and we even feel sorrow and pain when a tree that we have come to love sickens and dies or goes down in a sudden fierce storm.

To be appreciated, plants do not have to be personified. We need neither deify nor humanize them. We need only accept them gratefully in all their strangeness, as the alien presences that give us the means of life through their very being.

The proposition that plants have no intrinsic meaning for us in no way implies that we cannot *give* them meaning. Musical notes, in and of themselves, are mere vibrations in the air. Oil paints and tempera and watercolor in the abstract are equally meaningless. They are raw materials. Musical notes, those mere vibrations in the air, can become the Mozart *Requiem.* Dabs of paint transcend themselves when they become Botticelli's *Primavera,* Vermeer's *View of Delph,* or Picasso's *Guérnica.*

Bare of meaning for us in themselves, except for the hardly negligible point that they sustain our lives, plants become rich in meaning when we make a garden of them, choosing them for our own, arranging them in compositions that we find attractive, incorporating the nature that they represent into the substance of our lives. A jasmine or a rose, as it grows in the wild, says nothing to us, but in a garden it speaks volumes, for what we hear are the voices of gardeners from our very beginning. Like us, those ancient gardeners wished and needed to escape the human street and marketplace for a quiet, reposeful, lovely spot to call their own, where they might rejoice in green leaves and bright flowers during their seasons.

CHAPTER 9

How the American Suburban Landscape Came to Be

The way Hella and I have used the space where we have made our garden over many years is deviant—some of our neighbors might even say perverse. You can't see the front garden from the street, and if you could you would find no lawn there. We have no foundation plantings of evergreen shrubs. Elsewhere in town, with very few exceptions, the pattern is lawns out front and shrubbery corseting house foundations. We are scarcely aware of this pattern until some visitor from overseas calls it to our attention. When Hella's German cousin and her Austrian husband made their first visit to the States, they lost no time in commenting on the lawns open to the street, the foundation plantings, and the restriction of private space to the backyard, if there was any private space. "You Americans have so much room that you can waste it," they told us. "Where are your walls, your high hedges? And where are your flowers?"

Vita Sackville-West asked similar questions in *A Joy of Gardening* (1958), observing that Americans seldom planted hedges to shut themselves off from the inquiring gaze of passing strangers or to establish boundaries between their gardens and those of their neighbors. There was far too much openness, she believed, for we had "no sense of private enclosure," perhaps because we were "more brotherly-hearted" than our British cousins. She wondered if perhaps English gardeners might adopt the "democratic spirit" implicit in the American way of landscaping, but then expressed her doubts:

It is entirely at variance with our traditional idea that our own bit of ground surrounding our house, our home, be it large or small, is sacred to ourselves. Whatever our American friends may do, we shall continue to plant a hedge to block our immediate neighbors out, with much determination.

The most powerful ideas on earth are the unconscious ones that may have originated with a person or persons whose names we may not even know. Often we act upon these ideas, not really thinking about what we are doing, and not realizing that there may be more satisfactory ways of behaving. So it is with the suburban American landscape in which many of us live. It is not the product of some inevitable destiny. Mind—ideas—made it.

There is no great mystery about how the American suburban landscape came to take its present form, or about the ideas that went into its making. We must go back to the nineteenth century, and to prophets like Andrew Jackson Downing, Frederick Law Olmsted, and others who cried out for public spaces for public use—for green parks with great trees and winding paths and cooling ponds and, above all, vast expanses of well-kept lawn for every citizen to enjoy. In "The New-York Park" (1851), an essay published less than a year before his untimely death in a steamboat explosion on the Hudson River, A. J. Downing spoke of New York's "crowded hotels, crowded streets, hot summer, business pursued until it becomes a game of excitement, pleasure followed till its votaries are exhausted," and he pleaded for a great park in the city that would be "the quiet reverse side of this picture of town life, intensified almost to distraction." He argued that New York needed "broad reaches of park and pleasure-grounds, with a real feeling of the breadth and beauty of green fields, the perfume and freshness of nature."

This argument was, of course, highly instrumental in establishing Central Park, with its expanses of verdant lawn, but it also encouraged the idea of the lawn as a major element of residential landscaping. In another essay, published in 1846, Downing had observed, "There are but few good lawns yet in America; but we have great pleasure in observing that they are rapidly multiplying." Downing—

who is one of my heroes—never combined the lawn ideal with the notion that it should be open to the street, nor did he anticipate the invention of lawn mowers. (A lawn for him was something to be nibbled by sheep or shorn with a scythe!)

Ultimately, however, Downing was far less influential in shaping the way we live today in suburbia than was Frank J. Scott. His 1870 treatise *The Art of Beautifying Suburban Home Grounds of Small Extent,* which was dedicated to Downing's memory, breathed into the atmosphere the ideas that now inhabit the American mind and have a strong effect on how we plant our private property. Scott's influence was greater than Downing's for several reasons. He wrote at a time when new immigrants were flooding into the country, into the large cities in particular—and when old inhabitants were embracing the suburban ideal made possible by the new commuter railroads that enabled them to combine the advantages of working in the city with those of living in the almost-country. These new suburbanites were often uneasy about questions of social class. They no doubt were clear in their feelings of superiority to the new Americans living in the tenements along the railroad tracks they used to get to and from work every day of the week. I suspect that many of them were also a little concerned lest they in some way reveal their own immigrant origins. Such uneasiness always contributes to an outpouring of books of advice on how to seem to have arrived in society. This genre is old and enduring in our country. It includes Emily Post and Amy Vanderbilt and Miss Manners, as well as books like *Dress for Success* and magazines like *Architectural Digest.* Today we find continuing testimony to the etiquette of unease in that late-twentieth-century phenomenon Martha Stewart.

Scott had some firm ideas about what suburbia should be—an assemblage of private properties that would combine into a public space. If three adjacent neighbors each had an large stretch of lawn in front of their houses, with no barriers between them but with a few well-chosen trees, each neighbor would see from his front door a kind of parkland that all could equally enjoy. If the whole neighborhood was planted in this way, private ownership would contribute to public enjoyment. Furthermore, a family's suburban home ground would testify to all its good taste and position in society.

Today, Scott's ideas hold general sway in the land, but his prose occasionally makes amusing reading, as when he writes:

*F*rank J. Scott's Suburban Home Grounds *envisions an idyllic America where husbands work in cities to provide their wives and children with the advantage of country life—fresh air and verdant grass in a garden setting.* [SUBURBAN HOME GROUNDS]

A large and comfortable Victorian house complete with wide porches and gingerbread trim, expansive lawn planted with tall trees, and pleasant pathways for leisurely strolls—Frank Scott presented America with the suburban dream that still looms large in our consciousness.
[SUBURBAN HOME GROUNDS]

It is unchristian to hedge from the sight of others the beauties of nature which it has been our good fortune to create or secure, and all of the walls, high fences, hedge screens, and belts of trees and shrubbery which are used for this purpose are only so many means by which we show how unchristian and unneighborly we can be.

As for the old saying about high fences making good neighbors, he replied tartly that if people believed themselves to be bad people and thus bad neighbors, then they had a duty to fence themselves in. No such barriers were called for, however, in the case of "kindly gentlemen and women, with well-bred families." It is not difficult to fathom how this advice would have been taken in largely Christian nineteenth-century America, even if it now seems odd to find theological references in a discussion of home landscaping. But no one wants to be regarded as a bad person or neighbor, so Scott's argument still has its bite.

171

How the
American
Suburban
Landscape
Came to Be

Scott's ideas about how we should landscape our home grounds were not universally espoused. The novelist Sarah Orne Jewett lamented the passing of the dooryard gardens of New England, each with its lavish planting of flowers long loved and passed down from one generation to the next. In *Country Byways* (1881), she wrote that "people do not know what they lose when they make way with the reserve, the separateness, the sanctity of the front yards of their grandmothers." She added, "It is like writing down family secrets for anyone to read." Alice Morse Earle, in her 1901 classic, *Old-Time Gardens,* quoted Jewett approvingly. She also made the etymological point that "garden," "yard," and "orchard" are all derived from a word whose root meaning was a place enclosed, so that a garden open to the view of every passerby was inherently contradictory. Neltje Blanchan, writing in 1909 in *The American Flower Garden,* directly countered the notion that it was selfish or undemocratic to want privacy.

> In an emotional moment of "civic improvement" we were advised to take down our front fence and hedges, throw open our lawns, and share with the public all the beauty of our home grounds, or be branded as selfish and undemocratic. The family life that should be lived as much as possible under the open sky, when rudely exposed to public gaze, must become either vulgarly brazen or sensitively shy, in which latter case it withdraws to the vine-enclosed piazza or to the house itself. There is a vast difference between the Englishman's insultingly inhospitable brick wall, topped with broken

bottles, and an American's encircling belt of trees around his home grounds, or the tall hedge around his garden room to ensure the privacy without which the perfect freedom of home life is no more possible than if the family living-room were to be set on a public stage.

George Washington Cable, in *The Amateur Garden* (1914), made the same point as Alice Morse Earle—that in its very meaning a garden must be a place enclosed. He also made the telling observation that the poorer a family was, the smaller their lot would be, and the more likely that their neighbors would keep chickens who would damage plants.

The most damning criticism of Scott's ideas came after they had triumphed and were everywhere evident. In *Come Into the Garden* (1921), Grace Tabor, a landscape architect who wrote four books on gardening, remarked that our suburbs were—or "were said to be"—among the "most beautiful in the world," but she added a qualifier: "*to drive through.*" She made the sensible observation that a house and its grounds weren't public parks but homes for families. "They are not for the man who drives through" the neighborhood, but "for the man who stays there, and for his wife and their sons and daughters." Tabor complained that lawns open to the street were "wasteful, vulgarly frank and ostentatious, and utterly destructive of garden opportunities as well as of the fine instinct of home reserve and privacy that is such a priceless human asset." Although she recognized that Scott's ideas had passed from the marketplace of mere possibilities, with their alternatives, into law, with municipal ordinances everywhere restricting the height of fences and walls or even banning them entirely, she argued for a return to "older and better ways." Americans had made a fundamental mistake in landscaping their homes primarily to "capture the admiration of the street." She urged emulating the most common garden practices of other times and other lands by enclosing houses and gardens with walls right at our property lines. Instead of "a front porch overlooking the throng and the dust," a family would have an enclosed garden room, "where all the privacy and lounging indolence of indoors is possible, out under the blue in the fragrant sweetness of a true garden."

Grace Tabor did not mention Frank Scott by name in *Come Into the Garden,* but she clearly had him in mind and she realized that there was a "most serious error" in the philosophy of home landscaping that was his legacy. This error was "to treat the suburban grounds along the same lines which the large estate admits, to build the suburban house according to the same plans from which the house in the midst of acreage rises." Large properties might benefit from open landscaping that makes an elaborate mansion admirable at great distance from the street, but small properties needed to be set apart by walls or other visual barriers that bring privacy.

Tabor's ideas were not without their influence. They are perhaps best expressed and refined in the residential landscape architecture, primarily in California, that Thomas Church designed for his affluent clients. But elsewhere, in the suburbs inhabited by the less wealthy, Tabor's recommendation of walls and enclosure has had little impact.

By the 1920s, Scott's way of thinking had become ingrained in the American mind. Frank Waugh, a professor of landscape architecture at the state college in Amherst, Massachusetts, preached the gospel according to Scott. He also evangelized for another idea about how we should landscape our homes: the notion that houses must have their foundation plantings, must rise up out of the engirdling embrace of broadleaf evergreens and low conifers. Writing in 1927 in the introduction to Leonard H. Johnson's *Foundation Plantings,* Waugh sounded so much like one of the civic boosters that Sinclair Lewis parodied so wickedly that it is worth quoting him at considerable length.

> It is only fair to say that the home is the greatest institution in America—greater than the Republican party and the Democratic party combined—greater than any seven kinds of religious sects which might be named—more important than intercollegiate football—worth more to the country than votes for women. Now, the ideal American home means a single house for each family, with a little plot of ground, said plot to include a front yard between the street and the house with some sort of garden behind the house. This formula is universally accepted, even if not always followed. While it seems to be the trend of the times for more families to live in apartment houses,

173

How the
American
Suburban
Landscape
Came to Be

still nobody considers such an apartment a home. Much less do we look on it as the ideal American home. . . .

Everyone who is patriotic, therefore, and wants to do something for his country, will promote to the best of his ability the development of such American homes. It is well and sadly known, however, that tens of thousands of individual house lots have not been planted. We may all accept the further patriotic duty, therefore, of promoting this campaign of planting. In the Old Country, the primary planting which gives a home its individuality is a hedge all along the street front. The American home is characteristically different. The plantings, instead of forming a hedge on the street line, are pushed back against the foundations of the house. They are foundation plantings.

Probably by now it will come as no surprise that I believe that Scott and Waugh triumphed with a terrible idea, and that Sarah Orne Jewett, Grace Tabor, and all the rest in their camp lost with a fine and sensible one. It would be delightful if everyone in the country would immediately kill the grass in their front yards (or at least reduce its extent) and rip up half of the shrubs huddled against their house foundations and put them on the periphery of their property. I see nothing but good coming as a result. It would cut down on our use of fossil fuels to keep our lawn mowers going. It would reduce the staggering amount of herbicides and insecticides and fertilizers that are wasteful of energy as well as a threat to the safety of our groundwater, lakes, streams, and rivers. The human energy saved from the mindless task of mowing a lawn could be put to more important uses. People might begin to think about what they want to plant in their gardens, and soon the suburbs could be places where the narrow range of vegetation was widened enormously.

The sum of the individual parts of a neighborhood wouldn't add up to a public park—and they really don't, anyway. But they might add up to an arboretum, with a vast range of plants grown in a limited space, divided into rooms that would be as private as a dining room or a living room. I don't think this would be selfish at all. After all, we could always invite the neighbors over, and perhaps share plants with one another, thus building stronger and more intimate bonds than can be forged out of the fact that I mow my lawn, you mow your lawn, and that fellow over there, he mows one, too. And there's something else. Hedges need not be absolutely impenetrable. They can be loose enough so that a passing pedestrian catches a glimpse of some detail within the area they contain—the flash of a red peony or rose, the bright blue of a campanula, the tall red or pink or white spires of astilbes tucked into a shady corner. Any one of these sights, I think, is more beautiful to catch in a glimpse than all of the open lawns and foundation plantings in an entire city.

Anyone who wants to get some idea of what America might be like if we had followed Grace Tabor's notion of returning to the ancient tradition of enclosed gardens set off from the street need only pay a visit to the historic district of Charleston, South Carolina. Located on a peninsula between the Ashley and the

David Rawls's garden in the historic district of Charleston reflects some ancient gardening traditions that go back all the way to Rome. A quiet colonnade looks out on an atrium garden.

Rawls's garden, enclosed within walls of brick and stucco, features places to sit and read, paving, and a great many containers filled with both foliage plants and flowering plants.

Although many of Charleston's gardens are formal, and rely more on evergreen foliage than on flowers for their quiet appeal, the garden of Edward and Anna Crawford is abundant with flowering plants—larkspurs, salvias, climbing roses, and even Queen Anne's lace, ordinarily a roadside weed, but here given a prominent place.

Cooper rivers, Charleston is a walking city, one that holds together elements that other places, including its own sprawling suburbs beyond the two rivers, keep separate. In most of America, we sleep in one part of town, work in another, and go shopping in another. Charleston's suburbs could be suburbs anywhere—Dallas, Chicago, or Minneapolis. Frank Waugh would approve of them. Old Charleston, however, is different.

As a result of a severely depressed economy for many decades following the Civil War—a period in which local tradition has it that Charlestonians were "too poor to paint and too proud to whitewash"—progress passed the city by.

While the rest of the country built tall buildings and nourished the dreams of real estate developers who gave us suburbs that we could not possibly live in without cars, Charleston remained as it was—an old city built according to the ancient Mediterranean model of the juxtaposition of public and private places. Private residences intermingle with restaurants, office buildings, shops, and small inns. Churches—and there are many in the historic district, their steeples still the most prominent features of the city's skyline—are only a stone's throw from the offices of law firms and other businesses. The dead from olden times still rest in the city's cemeteries, adjacent to churches.

Today Charleston lives by tourism. Except when there are tours in the spring, the city's many private gardens are off-limits to the stranger and the visitor. Privacy is cherished, and it is protected here by high hedges and walls of brick, by wrought iron gates and fences. From the sidewalks, you can see only

179

How the
American
Suburban
Landscape
Came to Be

Visitors to Charleston who regret not being able to enter most of the city's private gardens have reason to appreciate Emily Whaley, for her garden is almost always open to the appreciative tourist. A small contribution is asked, which supports a number of Low Country charitable institutions.

Long having recognized that Charleston's soil is poor and very depleted, Patti McGee has made a splendid garden that takes the greatest advantage possible of containers.

bits of the city's gardens—the flash of red honeysuckle just beyond a gate, a crape myrtle or an oleander topping a fence and spreading out to cast some welcome shade on the public sidewalk, pots of geraniums and plumbagos on the wooden railings of the open porches or piazzas that are peculiar to the city's native architecture and grew out of the need to take advantage of the slightest ocean breeze in summer's sweltering heat and oppressive humidity.

Over the years I have made many friends in Charleston, so I have managed to enter those gates and see those gardens. Small and generally lawnless, they are little pieces of paradise, fragrant with jasmines and gardenias, filled with the music of splashing fountains that cool the air, colorful with subtropical plants such as brugmansias, gingers, and heliconias. Their ancient walls are covered with emerald mosses and sprout small ferns. Charleston has wretched soil, so much gardening takes place in containers, often set in gravel or standing on patios of sandstone or flagstone. Red bananas grow in huge terra-cotta pots, as do crinums, black elephant ears and the giant taro, tree ferns, rosemary, and bougainvillea.

Both house and garden are set apart from the street by their walls (although some houses front directly on the street with their gardens behind). Because they are set apart, they flow into one another, becoming complementary elements of a unified private and personal space. Old Charlestonians live in their gardens, not just in their houses. It is an intelligent and a pleasant arrangement, and it reflects an ancient wisdom that Frank J. Scott persuaded us to abandon, to our great loss.

181

How the
American
Suburban
Landscape
Came to Be

Part III

Gardening and the Spirit

Introduction

"Spirit" is an extremely rich and ambiguous word. Sometimes it is used to refer to a separable soul believed by some to survive the death of the body, or to refer to an angel or a demon, but those are not my meanings. Sometimes it is used interchangeably with "mind," but I wish here to stipulate a difference (meanwhile insisting, as I did at the outset, that I regard body, mind, and spirit as all referring to persons in their unity, not as parts of something else).

Mind, as I have used it in the preceding pages, means the activity of perceiving connections between external things or the objects of knowledge. Some languages have two or more words for knowing: Spanish, with *saber* and *conocer*, for example, distinguishes between impersonal and personal knowledge; German does something of the same with *wissen* and *kennen.* English is not so tidy. We may know the names of people down the street with whom we have never talked, but we also know our intimate friends. I shall make the distinction between impersonal and personal knowledge by treating the former as *knowing that.* I know that two plus two equals four, that water freezes at 32° F. and boils at 212° F., and that Europeans arrived in the New World in 1492. These are all examples of impersonal or objective knowledge.

In gardening, whether we know it or not, we are in a world of connections. A garden connects us to the world in many strange and wonderful ways, many of which are intellectual and have to do with facts. It connects us to history: every time we grow a potato, for example, we may be reminded of the conquest of Peru, and of the blight that caused the potato famine in mid-nineteenth-century Ireland that accounts for the Callahans and Cullinanes among us. Even a small garden owes much to far-flung places. Its hybrid fuchsias mingle the genes of *Fuchsia coccinea* from Brazil, *F. fulgens* from Mexico, and *F. magellanica* from Argentina and Chile. Its herbs come mostly from the Mediterranean basin. Tulips hail from Asia Minor, gardenias from southern Africa eastward to India, Malaysia, and China. Few gardeners ever know more than a small part of the original geographies of the plants they grow, but this knowledge provides genuine intellectual pleasure.

The spiritual pleasures of the garden have also to do with connections, but with experiencing them, rather than merely observing, perceiving, or knowing about them. It is one thing to know that E. H. Wilson risked his life in collecting *Lilium regale* in China, but it is another thing altogether to grow this tall lily with its fragrant, pure white trumpet flowers and to feel gratitude to Wilson for his gift to us and our gardens. He died in an automobile accident in 1930, five years before I was born, but one of his legacies blooms every June in my garden. It is a point of connection between us.

Feelings of thankfulness to others are not objective facts. They are feelings. The whole enterprise of gardening is shot through with feelings and affections—and these are spiritual things.

CHAPTER 10

Becoming a Gardener

When I was very young, at about the same time that I was struggling with long division, my mother decided that I should take piano lessons. One day in May, the teacher she found started with the basics, showing me middle C—first on the piano and then on a sheet of music. The teacher laid before me my future career as a pianist—finger exercises, Bach's Two-Part Inventions, and eventually (if I had the gift of genius and the knack of self-discipline), a debut at sixteen playing the Grieg Concerto in A Minor for Piano with the Dallas Symphony Orchestra! I never made it all the way to Grieg (though a friend did), or even to the second Two-Part Invention. I lacked talent, much less genius, and I was sorely deficient in self-discipline.

That same May, I started my life as a gardener. I was in the third grade, living just outside the tiny town of Irving, Texas, when a fourth-grade teacher named Mrs. Harkey enlisted me to work in her nursery, where she hybridized iris and daylilies. The first assignment she gave me was weeding part of her iris seedling patch. Like any novice, I was fearful of doing the wrong thing, such as pulling up a seedling instead of a weed. Mrs. Harkey reassured me with a piece of advice that has stayed with me ever since. "Irises," she said, "grow here in rows. Weeds come up where they please." She was right, of course. In gardening, there is a geometry not found in nature. This was only the first of many lessons that she was willing to teach a brand-new gardener. Mrs. Harkey initiated me into the mysteries of gardening and its almost endless pleasures. It was a seduction of sorts, and it changed my life, entirely for the better. I have been a passionate gardener ever since—and I'm speaking now of more than half a century.

People who don't garden and who are mystified by the whole enterprise are apt to misunderstand it. Nongardeners caught in the cross fire of conversation between two devout practitioners hear what they take to be highly technical language, partially in Latin, about *Milium effusum,* urea-form fertilizers, pH factors, double digging, and other matters. They may conclude that becoming a gardener is something like learning to play the piano. There is a starting point (the equivalent of finding middle C), there is a sequential order of things to be learned, and finally, there is the Grieg concerto—or discourse about *Milium effusum* (a European ornamental grass).

The wonder of gardening, however, is that *one becomes a gardener by becoming a gardener.* Horticulture is sometimes described as a science, sometimes as an art, but the truth is that it is neither, although it partakes of both endeavors. It is more like falling in love, something which escapes all logic. There is a moment before one becomes a gardener, and a moment after—with a whole lifetime to keep on becoming a gardener.

"Though a very old man," Thomas Jefferson wrote near the end of his life, "I am but a very young gardener." I think I know exactly what he meant. The young child who puts an okra seed in a pot of dirt, waters it, and then watches with fascination as it becomes a living plant, has as much claim to being a gardener as Russell Page or Christopher Lloyd. Furthermore, the end is present at the beginning, and the beginning at the end. That young child who plants his or her first seed senses intuitively that the act is significant for the future, a beginning of a committed way of life with rich and varied ramifications to come. Most experienced gardeners can tell you when and how it all started in their lives, what seed it was they planted—or who their own particular Mrs. Harkey was.

There is no single road into a life committed to gardening. One friend tells of her childhood frustration when her grandmother, an ardent gardener, gave her an iris and it died. "I decided just to forget about gardening," she says later, "and then when I was twenty I walked into a greenhouse in winter filled with flowers. That was it! I plunged right in, determined to learn as much about plants as I could in the shortest possible time." She is now a professional garden designer. Another friend tells of walking over the crest of a hill in Kentucky and being overcome by the beauty of a grove of buckeye trees in full bloom. A year later he was studying at Kew, and in time he owned a nursery. Some people start with a few tomato plants and some lettuce and end up as passionate collectors of orchids. The ways of becoming a gardener are many. It is, of course, possible to approach gardening systematically, taking a basic course in ornamental horticulture, learning about soil structure, chemistry, alkalinity, and such other things as whip grafting in their turn, while picking up the Latin necessary to identify plants in a way that is scientifically correct. Most of us, however, follow a more haphazard path. Comparatively few American gardeners major in horticulture in college. If asked, they will say they majored in English literature, Chinese history, art history, sociology—almost anything, it seems, is compatible with a passion for the garden.

The beginning gardener may find encouragement in one simple fact: there's very little that simply *must* be known in advance before someone can start becoming a gardener. There are some basic principles, of course, such as that plants need moisture, first to germinate and then to live. But how much moisture do plants require? It can be a lot or very little, depending on the particular plant. All knowledge about the requirements of a specific plant comes from experience. You can sometimes take advantage of the experience of others by reading a book (although not always, for garden literature is filled with half-truths and guesswork parading with authority on its sleeve). You can also learn from your own experience. "It died. I didn't give it enough water." Maybe. You might have given it too much.

It isn't the knowledge about plants and gardening that's of first importance. It's the passion.

Gardening is not a hobby, and only nongardeners would describe it as such. Hobbies are pastimes, diversions, and amusements. Each of these near synonyms carries implications of unimportance. A pastime occupies one's spare or leisure time in a pleasant way. A diversion entertains by distracting the mind, shifting its focus to something peripheral. The fairly shocking root meaning of "amusement" is to stare stupidly at something that lacks ultimate seriousness. People are interested in their hobbies because these activities are *their* hobbies, not because they are intrinsically important. Almost anything will do—collecting baseball cards or Barbie dolls, sailing, cooking Thai food.

There is nothing wrong with having hobbies, such as working on crossword puzzles on Sunday mornings or during long waits in airports, but most hobbies are intellectually limited and make no references to the larger world. By contrast, being wholeheartedly involved with gardens is involvement with life itself in the deepest sense.

My garden is peopled. Becoming a gardener means entering a world of deep and abiding friendships. I cannot walk into our garden without constantly being reminded of the friends who have shared their plants. This canna came from Doug, this iris from Edith, this especially fine perennial sunflower from Allen, and these hardy cyclamens from Nancy. I also know that plants from my garden grow in theirs—an unusually fine purple aster, a liriope with chartreuse leaves, a rare native gentian with bottle flowers of teal blue and apricot foliage in autumn. Some plants call up thoughts of friends not because they were gifts, but because we were together when I got them: Martha and Garry were with us when we found our pink brugmansia and our marvelous variegated hedychium, and Joanne and I both bought this pink canna at a strange little nursery in eastern North Carolina that we visited one hot afternoon in August.

Many of my plants come from mail-order nurseries, and there are some excellent ones in America today. Their owners almost never get wealthy from their business—a halfway decent living is the most they can reasonably expect—but they are moved by love of plants more than the prospect of financial gain, and they serve us all well in making it possible to grow uncommon and uncommonly good plants we otherwise would not have. It is always a sad day when a nursery we have come to depend on closes, when a Montrose Nursery or a Holbrook Farm goes out of business.

Some of the flowers we grow are hybrids, and I am grateful to their hybridizers, some of whose names I know. I am indebted to André Viette for 'Peach Fairy,' my favorite daylily. I didn't know Grant Mitsch personally, but he bred some wonderfully elegant daffodil cultivars; others, seedlings still identified by numbers and not named yet, I have from Brent Heath, who is a friend of many years. I am, of course, indebted, as I have mentioned already, to plant explorers like E. H. Wilson and my friend Barry Yinger, who in recent years has brought from eastern Asia so many splendid plants, such as *Angelica gigas,* and introduced them to American gardens. Again, my garden is peopled.

I know of no common interest that exceeds gardening as a source of lifelong friendships, nor as a means of making new friends almost constantly. G. K. Chesterton wrote somewhere that "fanatics soon find one another," and so it is among gardeners. Telephone calls and parcels fly back and forth between us. We exchange not only plants but also pieces of personal knowledge gained through experience, either our own or that of others. One friend tells me that she is extremely fond of the Tennessee coneflower, *Echinacea purpurea* 'Tennesseensis,' for its compact habit, its rather silvery pale pink flowers, and its petals, which are reflexed forward in an unusual and strikingly elegant way. But she has had no success in germinating it. Somewhat later, another friend tells me exactly what kind of cold treatment or stratification this coneflower requires to break dormancy, and I pass on the news. Yet another friend moves from New Jersey to the Gulf Coast of Florida. She calls regularly to chat about all the exciting new plants she can grow, as well as to lament her inability to grow a number of old favorites that need the chill of winter to survive. One day I mention to her my fervent desire to get hold of the violet-leafed giant taro (*Colocasia esculenta* 'Fontanesia') I have seen in an illustrated book on tropical gardening. A week later it arrives on my doorstep from Bradenton. Gardening is a web of relationships among people, as well as relationships between people and the rich world of plants.

I consider myself especially fortunate in having a family that shares my interest. Individual personal pleasure in the world of gardening is important, but it becomes deeper when someone dear and near at hand shares the pleasure. A gardening partner is a genuine benediction. The partnership ought to be even, if not entirely equal. Harold Nicolson gave Sissinghurst its bones, but Vita Sackville-West fleshed them out with wonderfully chosen plant combinations, and each delighted in the work of the other. I know more Latin names than Hella, but she sees more clearly than I when something is amiss, and she has a far better grasp of the principles of harmonious combination than I do.

I speak thus far of informal connections among gardeners, of a casual sort of horticultural freemasonry, but there also exist more formal, structured, and institutional associations. Today in the United States there are well over 200 local, regional, and national, organizations in which horticulture provides a bond among people. Some are of a general nature, but many serve the kind of particular passion that arises in people when they are especially smitten by one plant genus or by one kind of gardening. Daffodils, dahlias, and daylilies all have their national societies that hold conventions and sponsor newsletters or journals. So do hollies, passionflowers, and rhododendrons. Even gourds and chile peppers have their organized aficionados. The Seed Savers Exchange unites gardeners all across the country in the noble and important task of growing heirloom fruits and vegetables in order to preserve their valuable pool of genes. Rock gardening, aquatic gardening, and desert gardening all have their appropriate societies. America is also blessed with a multitude of botanical gardens and arboretums in almost every state. Many of these publish periodicals, sponsor talks by expert gardeners and plantsmen, and distribute choice plants to their members. Common among these institutions are groups of volunteers who help raise money and contribute their labor to keep things going. Personal friendships often arise among people who share an interest in the well-being of such public gardens.

The world of gardening affords more than communion among the living, as an interest in plants and in making a garden serves as a spiritual medium between the quick and the dead. Heaven has no area code or zip code that I know of, but still there is a kind of communication that goes on between those of us who still walk this earth and breathe its air and those who have gone on before us. I can read books by Canon Ellacombe, Celia Thaxter, Louise Beebe Wilder, Elizabeth Lawrence, Henry Mitchell, and many others among the saints gone to their rest with the sense that there is conversation between us. I can go back to Pliny and Horace with great enjoyment. I take special pleasure in reading the writings of the great English herbalists of the seventeenth century, John Parkinson and John Gerard, whom I have referred to or quoted at several points. Both writers were particularly wonderful when they were flushed with excitement over some new plant from a remote corner of the world that had just swum into their ken during the first days of plant collecting in the New World.

Take Gerard, for example, on *Mirabilis jalapa,* the four o'clock, which, as I have already said, was one of my favorite plants in childhood. We consider it old-fashioned, but to Gerard it was new, fascinating, and almost miraculous. His *Herball* devotes two oversized pages to it, commenting that although some people called it the marvel of Peru, he thought marvel of the world would be more like it. He noted that "the seed of this strange plant was brought first into Spain, from Peru, whereof it tooke his name Mirabilia Peruana or Peruviana." Gerard tasted the leaves, finding them "verie unsavorie," with a "taste and sharpe smacke of Tobaco." He wrote that the flowers resembled those of tobacco: "not ending in sharpe corners, but blunt and round." He found their fragrance "verie sweet and pleasant, resembling the Narcisse or white Daffodill." Their strange colors moved him to heights of admiration. But the most marvelous thing about the marvel of Peru was that one plant could bear flowers of several different colors and, what's more, that a single flower could be several colors at once—the same trait I found so wonderful as a boy. The flowers of *Mirabilis jalapa* behaved in ways entirely unaccustomed to Gerard, bringing something completely new into his experience: "two colours occupying half the flower, or intercoursing the whole flower with streakes and orderly streames, now yellow, now purple, divided through the whole; having sometimes great, sometimes little spots of a purple colour, sprinkled and scattered in a most variable order, and brave mixture."

When I read Gerard on four o'clocks I forget their familiarity: they become again a wonderful new discovery from the New World, seen through his eyes.

"We must cultivate our gardens." Indeed we must. A common interest in gardens offers a chance for rivalries to cease and peace to reign. America would be a happier place, I think, if all the presidents who came later had shared the horticultural passions of our third president—who after all traveled in France during the last days of the monarchy and in England between our two wars with her. In both countries he found gardens to admire, and like-minded persons with whom to correspond on matters of mutual horticultural interest. One thinks here also of the Empress Joséphine and her "peace of roses." Even when England and France were at war with one another and the French coast was under English blockade, the English nurseryman John Kennedy was permitted unimpeded passage back and forth across the Channel to deliver great numbers of rose plants to swell Joséphine's legendary rose collection at Malmaison.

Gardening transcends everything that otherwise divides us. Differences of religion, politics, nationality, ethnicity, gender, sexual orientation, and age become irrelevant among people of the gardening persuasion. The differences between the novice and the gardener with long experience become unimportant, for novices have set foot on the road they will probably follow the rest of their days, and experienced gardeners never cease learning (and never finish their gardens so they can say, "Now—it's *done*"). Gardeners gladly teach and gladly learn, as Chaucer put it. We are a friendly tribe and a generous one. We are spirited, we are alive to each day's new possibilities in our gardens, and on the whole we are men and women of good humor, perseverance, and forbearance.

CHAPTER 11

Connections to the Land

I have some ideas about the proper relation of gardeners to the land they work and tend. I do not believe they own it, except in the strict legal sense. I believe, rather, that they hold it in stewardship, that it is a responsibility, not a possession. Any piece of land at our disposal was here before we arrived, and it will be here after we have departed. The interim is ours, for making our lives and our gardens, and we must answer for both. At our departure, will we have used our patch of earth for its improvement and for the improvement of those who follow us, or will we have left things in a worse state than they were when we arrived?

In our ancient dream of controlling nature for human benefit, we do have some things to answer for. Shortly after the end of World War II, when my life as a young gardener had already begun, most American gardeners (my parents included) eagerly enlisted in an army with powerful new weapons at its disposal. Our enemies were no longer human ones, but the enemies of our home gardens, and they were legion and multiform. Some were weeds, like the dandelions that marred the smooth turf in spring or the crabgrass that spread like gossip later in the season. Some were insects—so many that it would take a Homer to catalog them all. But the gardener's world then was brave and new and filled with miracles and chemistry. There was 2, 4-D, for starters. Broadleaf weeds like dandelions had met their nemesis—a viscous liquid that turned the water used to dilute it a milky white. Sprayed on the offending weeds, it gave off a pungent, faintly nasty smell suggesting that it meant business. Shortly, the weeds went into visible agony, twisting into odd contortions before they finally died and dried up.

There were other new weapons against insects, including DDT and dieldrin and chlordane and others. All the garden columnists and practical books on horticulture dispensed expert advice on which pesticide to apply to which marauding caterpillar or beetle. Sometimes there were warnings as well, but these usually confined themselves to reminders not to use a sprayer that had contained 2, 4-D to put DDT on tomato plants, since the residual herbicide might doom them.

Gardeners felt that victory was at hand. We hoped as fervently as we had hoped for a vaccine against polio that dandelions and cutworms would soon become extinct. One book published in the mid-1950s on my mother's shelf of garden books promised that we could look forward to "an insect-free America." (Never mind that an insect-free America would be a starving America, considering the role of insects in pollinating many food plants!)

There were a few doubters, of course, led by J. I. Rodale, who founded *Organic Gardening and Farming.* An apostle of the compost heap, Rodale also lashed out at chemical fertilizers and pesticides, arguing that in our very effort to control nature for our benefit we were poisoning the earth—and ourselves. His passion made him suspect to some, who considered him a true believer (someone who first reached a conclusion and then went looking for anecdotal evidence to support it). Although his fundamental ideas about DDT and other pesticides proved sound, there was sufficient lunacy in his magazine on other matters to make it seem reasonable to dismiss his advice.

Then Rachel Carson came along with her sobering series of articles about pesticides in *The New Yorker* that were published in 1962 as *Silent Spring.* Carson had her critics, some of whom called her a crank and tried to dismiss her, as they had dismissed J. I. Rodale. But Carson was a professionally trained scientist, a marine biologist, and she was well respected for her best-seller, *The Sea Around Us* (1951). Furthermore, she had done her homework, assimilating technical articles in obscure journals in a variety of fields. She came to some very disturbing conclusions based on solid evidence, and in *Silent Spring* she presented them in terms anyone could understand. She talked of backyards where no robins appeared as signs of early spring, bird feeders where no birds fed, and eagles' nests where no eggs hatched. Then she explained the technicalities—such matters as the accumulation of toxic chemicals in the food chain and in the fatty tissues of individual living beings, including us.

Because of Rachel Carson and those who confirmed her evidence and conclusions—and those who heeded this new knowledge that controlling nature has its unsuspected, unintended, and most unwanted consequences—you can no longer buy chlordane to dust your tomatoes. The chemical feast, of course, continues: a visit to the pesticide section of the closest garden center testifies amply enough. But since J. I. Rodale and Rachel Carson, there are choices to make. We can live with insects and weeds, we can seek their total extermination according to the old programs of control, or we can decide where and how we will seek control and when we will not, meanwhile hoping that our choices will be wise—or at least not harmful.

Many people are now aware of the abundant environmental crises of our time: of deforestation in the tropics and in our own Pacific Northwest; of trees damaged or killed in the East from acid rain; of habitat loss; of possible depletion of the ozone layer; of pollution of water and air; of a growing crisis in agriculture as insecticides and new diseases seriously reduce populations of honeybees and other pollinators that many crops depend on. Such awareness typically is accompanied by a feeling of helplessness, even despair. But there is one place where a person can make choices that will lead in a small way toward greater sanity in dealing with the natural order. That place is the private garden. Lawns can be reduced in size or even eliminated altogether. Pesticides can be used more judiciously, or not used at all. In the vegetable patch, open-pollinated heirloom vegetables can be grown, thus helping preserve genetic material threatened by agribusiness and its reliance on F_1 hybrids. Gardeners who modify their own habits may not save the world. But at least they will not contribute thoughtlessly to its destruction, and they might even serve as examples of environmental wisdom to the larger community.

Hella and I are not organic gardeners of the strict persuasion, but we tend in that direction. We use no pesticides whatever indoors, where a vast jungle of plants crowds every window. We handle the occasional outbreak of mealybugs by ordering a couple of hundred *Cryptolaemus montrouzieri,* small Australian beetles that feed entirely on mealybugs in both larval and adult stages, from a company specializing in beneficial insects. From the same source we get *Metaphycus helvolus,* a tiny parasitic wasp that clears up infestations of brown-scale insects and other pests. Outdoors, we seldom resort to insecticides, and if we do, they are almost entirely botanical ones, such as rotenone and pyrethrum. To protect ourselves and the children who visit our garden, we do go on the offensive against wasps' nests. (On the deck, where we compete with yellow jackets for the same morsels of food, we use traps baited with fruit juice.) We use no broadleaf herbicides. We do use some contact herbicides. I sometimes use a strong solution of white vinegar to kill sidewalk spurge and other weeds that favor life between bricks and in crannies. I occasionally resort to Roundup (glyphosphate), although I'm not entirely sure that using it has no harmful consequences, as some of my friends insist: it breaks down quickly into harmless gases, but it may affect soil structure and tilth before it does. For the most part, we deal with weeds by weeding, in the knowledge that weeds will always be with us—especially nut-grass sedge, which even a flamethrower probably could not eradicate.

We seldom fertilize our tiny lawn. It's a mixture of drought-tolerant tall fescue and white clover, which with the assistance of nitrogen-fixing bacteria grabs the stuff from the air and converts it into a form that it (and presumably the fescue) can use as a nutrient. For the perennial borders and the great number of plants in containers on the deck and scattered through the garden, we do apply liquid chemical fertilizer on a regular basis. There's not much choice in the matter. About 100 years ago, someone planted a couple of red maples on our property as shade trees. Their voracious roots run everywhere, even upwards into large terra-cotta pots and wooden half barrels, where these are in contact with the soil. Frequent application of liquid fertilizer is almost a necessity under these circumstances. I apply a soluble 20-20-20 formula in the spring for a quick boost, followed by a high-phosphorus 8-59-9 formula, until the middle of August when fertilizing ceases for the year.

It is, admittedly, occasionally tempting to declare all-out chemical warfare against one pest—the slug. For most gardeners, the slug is the enemy incarnate. Moving by night on trails of slime, this repulsive, green-blooded mollusk works its mischief wherever it goes, leaving the leaves of hostas and other choice plants in tatters as it chomps its way through the garden, with its 27,000 tiny teeth in an organ called a raspula. Gardeners in other parts of the country should consider themselves lucky in one respect that they do not garden in the Pacific Northwest, where the banana slug—which can grow to ten inches long and weigh a quarter pound—holds sway. By comparison, the slugs inhabiting my garden are pikers, but there are far too many of them.

There are some harmless ways of reducing slug population. Strips of copper left lying about here and there repel them with a mild electric shock. Empty plastic beverage bottles with an inch or so of beer at the bottom will tempt them to drink—and drown. A little plate with a tablespoon of sugar and salt can be set outside at night, bringing them a ghastly death by immediate dissolution and dehydration. But these are halfway measures, almost appeasement. Were Monsanto or Dow to come up with something that would rid our garden of slugs, instantly and forever, I would be sorely tempted indeed.

A garden is not "natural," in the pure sense of the word. It is a creation of human making, of artifice. It is to some limited extent under the control of its maker or makers. I say to some limited extent because things happen in it and to it that are to varying degrees not within our control. Sudden windstorms come as they please, sometimes accompanied by hail. The first hard freeze may arrive early or late in the fall, the last early or late in the spring. There may be too much rain or not enough. Weed seeds float in on the wind, are excreted by birds on the premises, or hitchhike in with loads of manure or topsoil. Summer, more often than not, brings prolonged periods of high heat and humidity that encourage plant diseases. Early winter may see sudden plunges of temperature before plants have properly hardened off to withstand the cold. A plague of gypsy moths or Japanese beetles occasionally descends.

In a garden we may experience any of these things, all part of the processes of nature. We have no alternative but to accept them, even though we may find them unpleasant and not of our choosing. There will, however, be fair days as well as foul, and times when we may wish to step back and whisper to our garden, "You are so lovely." On such days, we know why we garden—why we wish to take a patch of land and invest our energy, our time, and our souls in the effort to make it beautiful and abundant of life.

CHAPTER 12

Time and the Gardener

Time, as we experience it in our daily lives, seems terribly important. We complain that there's never enough of it. We dislike anyone or anything that wastes it, and we're willing to buy almost anything that promises to save it for us.

Within the lifetimes of most of us everything has speeded up. We grab meals on the fly at fast-food restaurants that in no significant way restore us, and we are impatient if a line means a five-minute wait. We seldom write letters anymore. When a friend's birthday or wedding anniversary comes up, we resort to Hallmark. If we put a regular stamp on the card and mail it, we now call it "snail mail"—meaning it's not as important as something that comes by Federal Express. It won't be long before almost everyone in the country has a fax machine or uses the Internet. We haven't quite managed the metaphysical impossibility of being in two places at once, but we make do through electronics. We no longer have to be at home or at our office desks to receive phone calls. Voice mail or an answering machine takes care of them in our absence. If our work requires constant subservience to others, they can reach us on our beepers. If we have cellular phones, we no longer have to lose time while commuting to work. Laptop computers enable us to work on trains and airplanes.

Paradoxically, all of these conveniences serve to deny the reality of time by enabling us to overcome its limitations. The distinction between time to work and time to play is lost when we carry a cellular phone to a ball game or tennis court. Time becomes abstract, or it is manipulated in such a way that we lose all consciousness of it, all awareness that we are in it. Most casino gambling rooms have no windows and no clocks—no reminders of dusk or dawn. The shopping mall offers perpetual spring comfort inside, and the seasons merchants wish us to heed aren't spring, summer, fall, and winter, but the Christmas shopping season and the traditional times for special sales.

It is a bad thing, however, to believe that there is not enough time, or to forget about it entirely, for we are of all the creatures of this earth the most solidly situated in time. No other beings impose their order on the flow of time as we do. Calendars—and there have been many rival systems for making them—are our inventions. We number the years and the hours, give names to the months and the days. It takes but little reflection to realize that these numbers and names are purely arbitrary. No matter how firmly we may be convinced that sixty minutes by nature make up an hour and twenty-four hours a day, we might as easily divide the day into ten hours, each with 144 minutes. We unthinkingly believe that the first of January marks the beginning of another year, but other dates would do just as well. The Romans considered that a new year arrived in March—a defensible choice, since that month sees the first unmistakable signs of spring. The echo of the old Roman or Julian calendar is evident in the names we still use for November and December, which mean the ninth and the tenth month, although we designate by them the eleventh and the twelfth. The rhythms of calendars (and also clocks) do not precisely correspond with anything in nature. (In the Gregorian calendar we have to throw in an extra day in every year whose number is divisible by four, so that we in the Northern Hemisphere will not eventually find ourselves sunning at the beach in mid-December or making snow angels in July—and still, to make things come out right, we must skip leap year in those years ending in two zeros, unless they are divisible by 400.)

The rhythms that count—the rhythms of life, the rhythms of the spirit—are those that dance and course in life itself. The movement in gestation from conception to birth; the diastole and systole of the heart; the taking of each successive breath; the ebb and flow of tides in response to the pull of the moon and the sun; the wheeling of the seasons from one equinox or one solstice to another—these, not the eternally passing seconds registered on clocks and watches and not the days and months and years that the calendar imposes, define the time that is our true home and habitation, the time we dwell within until our own days are ended. If we lose consciousness of them, we become alienated from ourselves. I can think of no better place to overcome such alienation than a garden. Gardens, like we ourselves, dwell in time, and they do so in all its fullness.

If there are no daffodils in your garden and you wish to have them next spring, you must plant them in the fall. The act of planting daffodils and other spring bulbs in the fall is an act of faith, for you will not see the results of your work until the track of the sun has risen far enough toward its meridian to warm the earth and encourage growth. Then, to assure another bright time of daffodils in another year, the spent flowers must be removed so that the leaves may invest the solar energy produced by photosynthesis in next year's embryonic foliage and flowers rather than in seed. After daffodils flower, their leaves are sprawling, and unsightly, but no matter how strong the urge to tidiness may be, they should be allowed to ripen, for the sake of another spring to come. So it is with almost every plant. The cycles of the sun, of growth, and of the gardener's work according to season all coincide exactly.

Plants can tell time, as well as we can. Besides those morning glories and moonflowers that told the stages of a summer's day in my childhood, there are other plants of the day or the evening. The flowers of brugmansias or angels' trumpets first open at dusk, and older blossoms withhold their powerful scent until evening arrives once more. Most daylilies earn their name by opening at dawn. (A few wait until late afternoon.) Plants also know what season it is. Every gardener knows that June is the month of roses, that their bloom is most abundant then and that some roses bloom only then. We know not to expect chrysanthemums and New England asters until the autumn chill is in the air. If we are precision-minded souls, we may keep records of blooming periods as Elizabeth Lawrence did. A table at the back of her classic book *A Southern Garden* (1942) tells us that the earliest date for first flowering of the fernleaf yarrow in her Raleigh garden was May 22, the latest date was June 13, and that bloom was always over by July 31. She did the same for every flowering annual, biennial, perennial, shrub, and tree she grew. Thomas Jefferson kept similar records at Monticello. The convergent testimony of all such records demonstrates the ancient wisdom of Ecclesiastes: "To every thing there is a season, and a time to every purpose under the heaven."

Gardeners know that every plant has its season, according to its kind, but we may not know why this is. For such knowledge, if we wish it, we must turn to botanists and their explanations, which involve the co-evolution of all flowering plants with their pollinators. A wild ginger that bloomed in late summer rather than in late spring, when the fungus gnats that pollinate its odd, hidden, little jug-shaped flowers are abundant, would fail to produce the seed that carries with it the destiny of the species. Angels' trumpets that were fragrant by day, unperfumed by night, would advertise themselves unprofitably to the insects of the daylight hours, not the night moths (and possibly tropical bats) that spread pollen from one seductive flower to another. The blossoming of New England asters coincides with the migration of monarch butterflies from Canada to Mexico down the Atlantic flyway. Nature is everywhere synchronous, its individual parts so finely adjusted to one another that their harmony was once understood to be evidence of a Creator's hand. Some people still see it that way, even if others understand it as the beautiful logic of processes of co-evolution.

The most horrible life I can imagine would be one in which each day was the same as every other, in which we would get up at the same time every morning, work at the same tasks every day, eat the same foods at the same times, go to bed at the same time every night, and perhaps dream the same dreams between nightfall and the dawning of another identical day. It would not be life at all, but spiritual death, an existence in which everything is predictable. We would lose all humanity, becoming robots or automatons. We need our feasts and our fasts, our work days and our holidays, our sabbatical years and our years of jubilee. We need to wake up every morning with the sense that the day is new, conceivably miraculous.

In a well-made garden every day is new. There, our lives unfold with the passage of the seasons. When the first snowdrop lifts its milky-white blossoms in January, we know that despite the blizzard that's on its way, winter's grip cannot go on forever. When crocuses start to flower, we know that tulips cannot be far behind and that the time of roses is a promise that will be kept. Angry yellow jackets in August presage monarch butterflies in September, adding their graceful flight and their bright orange and black to the royal purple of the asters of gardens and meadows.

Brevity of bloom is not necessarily a defect in a flower. Occasionally people who aren't gardeners but who would like to have some flowers in their yards ask me what they should plant, then lay out their criteria of choice. They want something that is perennial, that they can plant once and then forget. They want it to grow in sun or in shade. They want it to be immune to disease and insect damage; to be able to go weeks without watering; to be a good cut flower; to come in many colors; and, above all, to be in bloom from the first good day of spring until the last good day of fall. If such people become gardeners, they will soon know that no plant on earth meets all these requirements. Those that come closest are annuals and very short-lived perennials. (Of these, the great majority—marigolds, gloriosa daisies, *Zinnia angustifolia*—are a hot shade of orange.) It is possible, of course, to make a garden primarily or even exclusively of plants that tend toward perpetual bloom during the growing season. The three that I have mentioned are suitable candidates, and you can add bedding salvias, impatiens, nasturtiums, petunias, pelargoniums, and a few other plants, all standard garden-center fare. A garden that consisted only of such champions of prolonged bloom, however, would lack the delights that come with much more ephemeral bloomers. Oriental poppies come into bloom and out of bloom in a very brief season indeed—less than a week in late May, unless it is unseasonably cool. Furthermore, an Oriental poppy out of bloom is not to be described as lovely. Its foliage is coarse and hairy, and its demise as it passes into summer dormancy is prolonged and ugly to behold. Bearded irises are among the most beautiful flowers of the garden—and my own first love, never to be forgotten as such—but once the first flowers have opened and begun to fade the plants are ragged-looking and fiercely untidy.

Peonies are also creatures of a brief season (although I find them lovely when their first red shoots poke up from the ground, consider their fat globes of buds supremely handsome, and enjoy their somber, dark green foliage all summer long). Passionflowers last only a day. But with none of these plants do I count brevity of bloom against them. A feast is no less a feast for not going on for weeks or months. (Who would want Thanksgiving more than once a year?) The loveliest flower I grow has in fact the briefest period of glory. It is a night-blooming cereus, a large, gangly, and ungainly plant that grows like a weed, sprawling out of its pot and shooting out new stems anywhere it pleases. (It's as rude as a puppy.). It blooms at most two or three times during the summer, never with more than three flowers at a time. They start opening at nine o'clock and by dawn they hang limply on their stems, somewhat reminiscent of strangled geese. But each flower is a miracle, more than making up for the undeniable defects of the plant, from the human point of view. The pure white, waxen blossoms inspire awe in their immensity and their stunning form that ravishes the eye and the admiration. It's a privilege to watch one of these flowers strut its sexual stuff, trying to lure the pollinator it's doomed not to find in New Jersey. It would not be better if a blossom stayed open forever: flowers of silk or plastic manage that trick very well, as is their nature to do.

A page or so back I wrote that in a garden every day is new. This is true, in the sense that each day brings something new to see, some slight change in the fullness of a flower or the turn of a leaf, but it is misleading unless the cycles of the gardening year are also kept firmly in mind. Gardens may have their history, as in fact every plant that grows in them has its history, but the gardening year is not really part of history. History, with its unique and unrepeatable events, like wars, the outcome of elections, and the ferocious and destructive storms that we assign human names, is lineal. The exact course of a hurricane cannot be known in advance. But the emergence of flowers on autumn crocuses in early September can be surely predicted. It happens every year, and it will continue to happen every year.

It is no wonder that so many people enjoy gardening. Political regimes rise and fall. Stock markets go up and down. The destinies and fortunes of nations and individual persons change according to events. A particular human being is born on one particular day and dies on another, as one small part of the history that moves in a straight and irreversible line from past to future. Gardening, however, is cyclical, except near the equator, where the length of days changes only slightly during the year. The position of the earth relative to the sun—and its tilt on its axis—gives those of us who live in the temperate zones a circle of seasons, from solstice to solstice, equinox to equinox. Allowing for minor variations, we know that winter will be cold and summer hot, that spring and fall will be variable but always serve up for us some days that are just perfect.

We know furthermore that tulips and hyacinths will bloom in April and May, that in July and August the roadsides will be brilliant with chicory and black-eyed Susans, and that in September and October chrysanthemums will bloom—and that winter will come on as the bright season departs.

There is a rhythm to the gardening year, much like the liturgical year of the Christian calendar, in which Advent always precedes Christmas, and Easter always follows Lent. The liturgical calendar invests chronological time with spiritual meaning, and so does the calendar that gardeners live by. We live and work in harmony with a cycle of changing seasons that is not of our making. It is the product of latitude and longitude, of our own particular place on earth, and of the movement of our planet around the star that gives it light. In making a garden, we must pay heed to larger, completely predictable events that are entirely beyond our control. Outside the cyclical world of the garden lies history, in whose fabric our own lives are enmeshed but not entrapped.

To garden is to be spiritually connected, and it means that we must submit, in true humility, to nature and its great wheeling cycles, its circles of seasons. For there to be harvest, there must first be seedtime. The prodigality of summer is balanced by the fallow time of winter. Little in a garden can be hastened, for the seasons cannot be altered.

Wars and hurricanes happen, but the hardy cyclamen in my garden will put up fresh new leaves one October after another. This event, just one of many that take place in a garden in the course of a year, is a species of eternity. It helps explain why all gardeners know that the work they do is good for their souls.

Select Nursery List

Fortunately for gardeners in search of particularly choice plants, America is blessed with a large number of splendid and entirely reliable mail-order nurseries. Because they serve a national clientele rather than merely local customers whose tastes run to the most common annual bedding plants, a limited number of perennials, and staple woody plants, these mail-order nurseries can offer rare and unusual plants not easily found elsewhere. New nurseries keep springing up, and—unfortunately—excellent ones like Montrose Nursery and Holbrook Farm, both in North Carolina, go out of business.

A new resource for gardeners looking for plants by mail is the World Wide Web of the Internet. An ever-enlarging number of nurseries have their entire catalogs available here, often with color photographs of their offerings.

What follows is my personal list of favorite nurseries from which I have ordered repeatedly, always with satisfaction.

CANYON CREEK NURSERY, 3527 Dry Creek Road, Oroville, California 95965. Catalog $2.00. Canyon Creek puts out a delightful catalog for bedtime reading. Specialties are dianthuses, hardy fuchsias, and violas.

THE DAFFODIL MART, 7463 Heath Trail, Gloucester, Virginia 23601. Catalog free. Despite its name, this long-established firm sells all kinds of bulbs.

FAIRWEATHER GARDENS, Box 330, Greenwich, New Jersey 08323. Catalog $3.00. Fairweather specializes in uncommon woody plants of special merit. It ships substantial plants, not mere rooted cuttings, and the packing is exemplary.

FORESTFARM, 900 Tetherhod, Williams, Oregon 97544. Catalog $2.00. Forestfarm sells sizes of rare woody plants at very reasonable prices. Patient gardeners can grow them on to size in their own nursery beds and eventually transplant them into their permanent locations.

HERONSWOOD NURSERY, 7530 288th Street, Kingston, Washington 98446. Catalog $4.00. Heronswood's thick catalog is the richest I have yet seen. There is a vast offering of deciduous and evergreen woody plants as well as extremely uncommon herbaceous perennials, including cultivars of British and European origin that few other American nurseries offer.

KLEHM NURSERY, Route 5, Box 197, South Barrington, Illinois 60010. Catalog $4.00. The specialties here are daylilies, hostas, and peonies, but in recent years the nursery has branched out into offering a great many other perennials.

PLANT DELIGHTS NURSERY, 9241 Sauls Road, Raleigh, North Carolina 27603. Catalog $3.20. Tony and Michelle Avent's remarkable nursery well outside the city limits of Raleigh is open to the public on designated weekends during the growing season. There is a fine selection of dwarf conifers here, as well as many perennials of East Asian origin, including hostas.

SANDY MUSH HERB NURSERY, Route 2, Leicester, North Carolina 28748. Catalog $4.00. Culinary and ornamental herbs and many scented pelargoniums are the primary offerings of this nursery in the Smoky Mountains west of Asheville.

SHEPHERD'S GARDEN SEEDS, 30 Irene Street, Torrington, California 06790. Catalog $1.00. Founded in California by Renee Shepherd, this company features seeds of heirloom vegetables and antique flowers, as well as unusually tasty vegetables of European and Asian origin. The catalog provides many delicious recipes and charming line drawings and watercolors.

SISKIYOU RARE PLANT NURSERY, 2825 Cummings Road, Medford, Oregon 97501. Catalog $2.00. Siskiyou is a fine source for alpine plants and native American shrubs.

ANDRÉ VIETTE FARM AND NURSERY, P.O. Box 1109, Fisherville, Virginia 22939. Catalog $6.00. This is one of America's leading perennial nurseries, with ample listings of daylilies, irises, hostas, Oriental poppies, and peonies. There are beautiful display gardens with a fine view of the Blue Ridge Mountains.

WOODLANDERS, 1128 Colleton Avenue, Aiken, South Carolina 29801. Catalog $2.00. Woodlanders deals mostly in woody plants, with an emphasis on those native to the southeastern United States.

Bibliography

Austen, Ralph. *A Treatise on Fruit Trees.* London, 1653. Reprint. New York: Garland, 1982.

Bartram, William. *Travels through North and South Carolina, Georgia, and East and West Florida.* London, 1792. Facsimile edition. Charlottesville, Va.: University Press of Virginia, 1980.

Betts, Edwin Morris. *Thomas Jefferson's Garden Book.* Philadelphia: American Philosophical Society, 1944.

Bodanis, David. *The Secret Garden.* New York: Simon & Schuster, 1992.

Cable, George Washington. *The Amateur Garden.* New York: Scribner's, 1914.

Clarkson, Rosetta. *Green Enchantment.* New York: Macmillan, 1940.

Creasy, Rosalind. *The Complete Book of Edible Landscaping.* San Francisco: Sierra Club Books, 1982.

Eck, Joe. *Elements of Garden Design.* New York: Henry Holt, 1995.

Dallimore, William. *Holly, Box, and Yew.* London, 1908. Facsimile edition. London: Minerva Press, 1978.

Downing, Andrew Jackson. *The Fruits and Fruit Trees of America.* New York: John Wiley, 1845.

———. *Rural Essays.* New York: Leavitt & Allen, 1854.

Earle, Alice Morse. *Old-Time Gardens.* New York: Macmillan, 1901.

Farrer, Reginald. *The Rainbow Bridge.* London, 1926. Reprint. Little Compton, R.I.: Theophrastus, 1977.

Gerard, John. *The Herball, or Generall Historie of Plantes.* Second edition. London, 1633. Facsimile edition. New York: Dover Books, 1975.

Irving, Washington. *The Alhambra.* New York: Putnam, 1889.

Jekyll, Gertrude. *Home and Garden.* New York: Longmans, Green, 1900.

Jewett, Sarah Orne. *Country Byways.* Boston: Houghton Mifflin, 1881.

Keller, Helen. *The Story of My Life.* Garden City, N.Y.: Doubleday, 1903.

Lawrence, Elizabeth. *A Southern Garden: A Handbook for the Middle South.* Chapel Hill, N.C.: The University of North Carolina Press, 1942.

_____ . *Gardens in Winter.* New York: Harper, 1961.

M'Mahon, Bernard. *The American Gardener's Calendar.* 11th ed. Philadelphia: Lippincott, 1857.

Parkinson, John. *Paradisi in Sole: Paradisus Terrestris.* 1629. Facsimile edition. London: Methuen, 1904.

Sackville-West, Vita. *A Joy of Gardening.* New York: Harper, 1958.

Scott, Frank J. *The Art of Beautifying Suburban Home Grounds of Small Extent.* New York: D. Appleton & Co., 1870.

Spondberg, Stephen. *A Reunion of Trees.* Cambridge, Mass.: Harvard University Press, 1990.

Tabor, Grace. *Come Into the Garden.* New York: Macmillan, 1921.

Ward, F. Kingdon. *Plant Hunting at the Edge of the World.* London, 1930. Reprint. London: Methuen, 1974.

Waugh, Frank A. Preface to Leonard H. Johnson, *Foundation Planting.* New York: A. T. Delamare, 1927.

Wilder, Louise Beebe. *The Fragrant Path.* New York: Macmillan, 1932.

Wilson, Ernest H. *A Naturalist in Western China, with Vasculum, Gun, and Camera.* London: Methuen. 1913.

Index

Boldface page numbers indicate photographs or other illustrations.